MW00711885

Been Married All My Life...
Never Had a Husband

Shirley W. Hines

This book is based on a true story.
The names have been changed to protect the innocent.

Been Married All My Life...Never Had a Husband

Copyright © 2007 Shirley W. Hines. All rights reserved. No part of this book may be reproduced or retransmitted in any form or by any means without the written permission of the publisher.

Published by Wheatmark™
610 East Delano Street, Suite 104, Tucson, Arizona 85705 U.S.A.
www.wheatmark.com

ISBN: 978-1-58736-796-0
LCCN: 2007921578

Acknowledgments

First and foremost, I must thank God for blessing me to complete this book. It was He who placed the inspiration for the book in my spirit and provided me with all the necessary tools I needed to complete it. Without Him, I could not have accomplished this or any other thing in my life. Second, only to God, I must thank my dear, wonderful husband Timothy. Meeting and marrying him has been one of the most wonderful things that has ever happened in my life. He has been in my corner from the very start. His love, strength, faithfulness and dedication has always kept and continues to keep me grounded and focused on striving to be the very best that I can be. Then I must thank my wonderful children Thomas, Shirletta, Myron, James, and Malik. They are a major part of my life. I want them never to forget that my life would be a very empty, desolate place without them in it. They've made and continue to make my life very blessed and interesting indeed. Then there are my dear sisters Edithphine and Darlene. They have been my most faithful cheering squad for a long, long time and they continue to be my faithful cheering section. I thank and appreciate them so much for encouraging me from the very beginning of writing this book. I thank them for their constant, unconditional love and support that only sisters can give. I love you both. I must thank my dear brothers, James and Daniel. They have encouraged me and given me their blessings with writing this book, as well as other of my life's endeavors and I love them very much. I must also thank Gwendolyn Jones and my sister Darlene for taking the time out of their very busy schedules to provide me with editorial services. I must thank Gwendolyn Jones and Dr. Jones-Taylor for taking the time out of their very hectic schedules just to give me uplifting words of encouragement and support. Thank you Phyllis for the cute little notebook that has proved very helpful indeed. It has helped me to organize the many, many notes I kept. Thank you to all of my co-workers that wished me well with my first book-writing experience. Last, but certainly not least, I must thank all of the readers that found an interest in my book and took the time out of their busy schedules to read it. May God richly bless you all.

Chapter 1

The farthest I can remember back from the very start of my life is around the age of four. I remember being at home with my mom while my three older brothers and two older sisters were in school. The highlight of my day was lunch time. My dad came home promptly every day at noon for a hot lunch that my mom faithfully prepared. My dad always came home with a little brown bag in his big ole hands, filled with cookies and candies. I loved all the attention I received from my mom and dad in my older siblings' absence. I remember this being a genuinely happy time in my life. Then it became my time to start along this long road beginning with kindergarten. My little quiet, serene life changed abruptly. I'm from a very small, close knit town in Virginia and this kindergarten idea was just being implemented in our little city the very year I started. It was a complete shock at first when my mom walked me to school, which was right down the street from our house, on that first morning. Then, to make things worse, she left me there encompassed by a group of total strangers. After I settled down emotionally and my big ole eyes returned to their normal largeness, I decided that this might not be so bad after all. There were lots of games, toys, other kids, coloring stuff, snacks, lunch, we watched movies, played outside, and then we took a nap. We learned as well. This kindergarten thing turned out to be a pretty cool idea. Just when I was thoroughly relaxed and enjoying kindergarten, I was introduced to first grade.

Well, just like any other morning, my mom, Ethel, walked me and my sisters, Evelyn and Doll to school. When mom walked me to my class, there in that room was a very nice teacher, about fifteen other little people, desks everywhere, a chalk board, books; but no really neat stuff. Where were the mats, the toys, games, and snacks? What happened to movie time and nap time? This just must be some great mistake? As it turned out, the only person that was mistaken was me. I had to sit at a desk, sit still, listen to the teacher and not interrupt her when she was speaking, lift my hand if I needed something. I was not feeling this in the very least. Every morning, for almost 2 weeks, I'd escape from the room by asking to use the restroom. After becoming nauseated every morning, I mean genuinely nauseated, the teacher would excuse me. After leaving the classroom, I'd run home as fast as I could, only to be retrieved by none other than good ole mom, and escorted right back to my classroom. Well, needless to say, I finally figured that there was no point in losing a perfectly great breakfast on the sidewalk leading home, only to have to return right back to class on an empty stomach. I stayed in school thereafter. I actually begin to enjoy school. I loved to learn new things, new ideas. It was pretty cool.

As I reached higher grades in school, I found that school was good, but children could be pretty cruel. I genuinely loved this girl named Bertha Powell. Being raised in a Christian home where we were taught to love everyone, turn the other cheek and all of that, I thought that people genuinely loved me as well. How mistaken I was. I would share my change with Bertha, invite her to our home in the evenings and cook my dad's finest T-bone steaks for her. I really thought she was a great friend. Later in 7th grade, I saw what a mean person she really was. She would get together with her cousin who was also named Bertha and taunt me endlessly and mercilessly. Me, being my little sweet, forgiving, loving self, would forgive her and continue to try to be her friend. This did not work. I really didn't like her cousin Bertha. She was very mean and she was ugly, both inside and out. I remember one day in Art class, her cousin Bertha pushed me very hard, almost causing me to fall. Well, cousin Bertha had obviously been misinformed by my so called friend Bertha that I was just a pushover. How misinformed cousin Bertha was. I shoved her right back, just as hard, or harder than she shoved me. Cousin Bertha left me alone from that day to this one. I left my mean friend Bertha alone as well. I became somewhat of an introvert from that point on. I found it much more comfortable to entertain myself with reading, writing, playing, whatever, than to run the risk of being hurt again by someone that I held to be a close friend. Being a loner was much more of a safe place to be. I still remained friendly but once at home, I enjoyed not having to be friendly.

I was a very happy child at home those first 13 years of my life. Mom and Dad had been married for ten years before they were able to have children. They wanted children so much and mom always told us we "were prayer children." Even though they kept us in church every time the church doors opened, I loved church. I enjoyed watching as some of the ladies and a few of the men would start shouting. I remember that if I was sitting behind someone and they started shouting, I instinctively ducked. They would be flapping their hands and arms all around, jerking what seemed to me to be uncontrollably. I was sure that lift-off was eminent. I remember on several occasions, some of the ladies would shout until their wigs went flying right off their heads, landing in a heap on the floor. Most of the ladies hair would be a real mess. Some of them would have what seemed to be millions of tiny plats underneath those wigs. This was real entertainment for me. I would have to run to the bathroom sometimes so that I could laugh as hard as I wanted to. On other occasions in church, things were not so funny. I can remember that every time the prayer line was called, my dear, sweet mother, who would always sit in the very front of the church, would look back at us. She would have the sweetest smile on her face as she beckoned with her warm eyes for us, her little angels, to come up and get into the prayer line. We would look right back at her, just as warmly and sweetly as she looked as us, while turning our heads from side to side meaning, no thanks mom. She would again look at us with those warm, gentle eyes and that sweet smile on her face, urging us to come up for prayer. She would mimic, "come on now, come on up for prayer." We would again give her that sweet, winning look only children know how to give to their parents, in hopes that she would turn around and drop the subject completely. Well, after that second exchange, something happened. That sweet, warm smile and kind look in mother's eyes, turned into something quite different all together. The smile on her face was transformed into a grimace and the kind eyes turned into nothing more than two small glints. She would use her index finger to motion to us as if to say, "if you all don't get up now and get in this prayer line, when I'm finished with you, you're really going to need prayer." Needless to say, there would be six children lined up, waiting for prayer, and when we returned to our seats, I can't speak for my siblings, but I was filled with more of the devil than anything else. If judging from their looks was any indication, they were all feeling the very same emotions as me.

Mom had a twin sister, Aunt Rae. They were not identical twins and they didn't look much alike to me. They were not alike in some mannerisms either. Mom was a home body and she loved her children to the point of being overly protective. She hardly went anywhere but church and church functions. Aunt Rae, on the other hand, was a free-spirit. She never missed an opportunity to get dressed to the tee and go wherever she wanted to go. She loved to strut in those high heeled shoes and she could strut too. She, to this day, still struts her heels. She loved to travel and did so constantly. Both sisters were very wise and prophetic, but Aunt Rae had worldly knowledge too; mom did not. Every summer, Aunt Rae's children, all seven of them, would come down for a summer visit. I enjoyed them and I loved to hear them talk. They lived in Brooklyn and their accent fascinated me. We were always very close to Aunt Rae and her children. She, like mom, married a preacher. His name was Uncle Robert and he was a very sweet man with a very humble spirit. Aunt Rae's sons were very busy and they loved to run wild in the country as they termed it. They all nicknamed dad "The Bear" because of his deep voice and stern disposition. The girls were and still are very sweet. Hart, the youngest was my hanging buddy when we were all together. She always spoke her mind and she was very stubborn but I enjoyed being around her because she was still very sweet. Before the end of their visit, they would all be ready to go back home because "The Bear" was so strict and thought nothing of giving them a beating just as quickly as he would whip our behinds. We had an aunt and two uncles on my father's side of the family. I remember as a child, I was very close to Aunt Mary but it seemed we grew apart as I grew older. It was said that I looked just like her. I was really close to her husband, Uncle Tim though. He was a giant of a man but he was as mellow and sweet as he could be. I wasn't really close to my Uncle Paul. I guess it was because he lived in Miami although he was as sweet as he could be the few times he visited us. My Uncle Wesley was a whole different issue. I loved him dearly. He would always come to visit us and each time he saw me, he gave me a kiss and held me on his lap the entire visit. He always called me his little Sweetheart. He was the total opposite of dad. He had the mildest demeanor in the world. He died when I was about fourteen or fifteen years old I guess, and even though I was a young teen, I remember his sickness and untimely death. He had emphysema and I remember going with dad to the VA hospital in Richmond to visit him. He just lay there in that hospital bed, totally unaware of our presence. I was very young but I remember how lost I felt at his funeral. I knew that I would never get to sit on his lap again. I've always been close to Uncle Wesley's family as well. They were always very sweet and down to earth people. My cousin Mae would and still will give a person the shirt off of her back if she thought they needed it.

Chapter 2

My life after the age of 13 seemed anything but happy. My father, John Lee White, Sr., had always been a very stern, strict disciplinarian with a very deep voice. These things about him never really bothered me until I reached that ripe, adolescent age where I began to have my own thoughts and ideas about life. I can remember that he always seemed more than happy to give us girls the beatings of our lives whenever my mom chose to remember to tell him what mischief we had been up to on any particular day. I swear Dad could take his belt off faster than Zorro could make a Z with his sword. My eldest brother, John Jr. suffered with asthma, so I really cannot recall him getting any beatings. My next to the eldest brother, Orlando, was always a challenge and I think now that Dad feared him. I can remember Orlando, who was 10 years my elder, coming in late, drunk and vomiting all over everything. He would offer to fight my mom and dad if they said anything to him. He would offer to fight them when he was sober as well. I remember my dad rarely getting into any confrontations with Orlando. My mom, on the other hand, was a very different story. Ethel Mae was a very soft spoken woman. She had a hearing deficit that stemmed from untreated pneumonia as a child and she wore a hearing aid that made loud buzzing noises. I think the thing buzzed more than it aided in her hearing. Nonetheless, whenever my mom was angered, she lost all fear of everything and anyone. She would not back down from Orlando and he knew it. As badly as he behaved as a teenager, he would seldom give mom any real threats.

My youngest brother David was a really cool guy. He was very quiet and laid back. He never got into any confrontations with any of us. He was always to himself or running like a wild man in our huge back yard or shooting hoops. As I saw it, dad always focused on us girls, mainly Evelyn and me. He rarely gave Doll any beatings. He called her his "Christmas Present" because her birthday came one day after Christmas. As a matter of fact, Evelyn and I were always made to clean the entire house. This included the laundry, waxing and buffing the hardwood floors, dusting all of my mom's millions of little glass decorations, and the cooking. We would ask that Doll clean the bathroom. We had only one little bathroom for a household of eight people. Looking at it now, I wonder how we all managed with that set up, but we did. Well, Doll would take all day long to clean that one little bathroom. As we later learned, she would sit there and read all day long as Evelyn and I cleaned and cleaned until we were drop dead tired. I asked Doll about this since we've been grown and she said, "I've always liked to read because reading took me to places that I've always dreamed of going. I knew I was not going to stay in this small town. As soon as I was grown, I knew that I would leave to see some of these far away places that I read about." I was like, yeah, but what did that have to do with you helping Evelyn and I clean the house before 5:00 pm?

Looking back on this period in our lives, I really cannot recall Doll ever cooking any meals. This favoritism that my father showed toward Doll made a big difference in the way Evelyn and I treated her. We would gang up on her and fight her and do little mean things to her out of direct retribution of our Father's indifference. I think Evelyn felt more strongly toward doing Doll in than I did. Evelyn later told me, "The reason I used to try to wipe her out was because daddy would look at me and say, look at you. You look like a Sour Puss. Look at Doll. She's always smiling and she's prettier than you are. She's my Christmas present. I love her more than I do you." Evelyn says those words from dad made her dislike Doll a lot as a child.

I loved both my sisters even though I would team together with Evelyn and pick on Doll. I would defend Doll if anyone else messed with her though. This was not the case with Doll concerning me. The home town girls would always pick on my sisters and me. They would tease us unceasingly, calling us big eyed and ugly. We were never girls that just randomly picked on anyone so we never understood why we seemed to be so disliked by the general population of our small town. I remember once on the school bus coming home, this big, tall, fat girl with very short hair was picking on Doll. She was calling her all kinds of ugly little names. My sister Doll would not say anything back to her. I, on the other hand, was always one to take up for and protect my sisters. I told her, "Leave my sister alone." She immediately started in on me. She said, "Since you're so bad, meet me when we get off the bus." I replied, "I will." I told Doll, "Let's get her at the bus stop." Well, when I got off the bus stop, this big, giant of a girl immediately begin to beat my butt, royally. She just stood there with her hands perched on her massive hips, allowing me to throw all kinds of punches to her huge mid-section. Then when she seemed bored with my unfruitful attacks, she would throw one huge punch that knocked me on the ground. When I shook it off, which took several minutes, I would repeat this scenario, only to be knocked almost senseless to the ground again. I looked around for Doll and all I could see of her was her little yellow dress in the wind, and her running as fast as her bony legs would carry her in the direction of our house. Well, this attack went on until my Mom and Evelyn came running up the street to rescue me. I had never been so glad to see my Mom and Evelyn before in my entire life. I later wondered why Doll would allow me to take up for her and get the stuffing beat out of me without helping me. Wasn't it her fight initially anyway? I did realize something very important that day. I was a lot like my mom, fearless to a fault, no matter what size the challenge.

Chapter 3

My Dad made my home life anything but enjoyable in my early adolescent years. He fussed from the time he got up in the mornings, then, he would resume his fussing as soon as he walked in the door from work. He would fuss at Mom without cease, and about nothing to the smallest of things. I feel Mom's hearing loss was a blessing to her sometimes. He was a deacon in the church and the most he smiled at us was while sitting in church. Whenever he'd look over and flash one of those prize winning smiles, I wanted to throw up. That made me sick. As soon as we would all pile back into his Buick 225, he would immediately resume fussing. Later, Dad was ordained as a Pastor, and a few years later; he was ordained as a Bishop. He would then flash that prize winning smile at us from the pulpit. I remember that some of his sermons even seemed fussy. I remember this one deacon that sat on the front row in the church. This poor guy would make the mistake of nodding off during one of Dad's sermons. Well, my Dad would literally jump out of the pulpit and go over to this poor man and startle him awake. He would tell

him, "Wake up brother, how are you going to hear the word
asleep?" He jumped out of the pulpit at us girls a few times as
well. Evelyn, Doll and me would be sitting in the congregation
talking to our little friends. Church services would last from
Sunday school, which started around 10:00, until late in the
afternoon, around 4:00 or 5:00. We would be bored to tears,
so we would entertain ourselves with the other girls in the
church. Well, Dad would not hear of this. He would interrupt
his sermon, jump out of the pulpit, take that Zorro belt off and
beat us right there in church in front of everyone. He would
then go back up in the pulpit and talk for a moment about how
he would discipline his children wherever they acted out at.
Needless to say, we were as embarrassed as we could be but
we knew better than to keep crying. One thing I never understood and still to this day, I do not comprehend is, Dad would
give us the beatings of our lives, and if we didn't immediately
start to cry, he would say, "Oh, you're not going to cry huh?"
Then after we started crying and screaming bloody murder,
he would say, "shut up before I give you something else to cry
for." You go figure.

My brothers rushed to leave home as soon as they graduated high school. They wanted to get away from my Dad's
fussing and overly dominating ways. My brother Orlando
robbed a bank near our small city and that worried my mom
almost literally to death. I remember when she first heard the
news. She had just prepared a bowl of soup for herself. After
the police left our house, she never even thought about that
soup any more. She just got in bed and stayed in bed for what
seemed to be almost a month or a little more, not eating or
anything. The police could never catch Orlando because he
was really, seriously a genius or very close to it. So the FBI was
called in. I remember two of them coming to the house and

mom begging them not to kill him. Then Orlando called the house one day from Brooklyn. The FBI had cornered him near Aunt Rae's house and he ran and ended up jumping off of an eight story building in bedroom slippers without getting as much as a scratch. I'm sure now that while mom was lying in that bed, she was crying out to the Lord to protect her child. Anyway, mom pleaded with him to turn himself in and that is exactly what he did. He was sentenced to twenty-five years in prison and he served ten of them. We went to see him very often. Mom would cook and bake all kinds of great foods to take for him and us. That was a very sad time for us all. My sister Evelyn enlisted in the Army as soon as she graduated as well. Doll became pregnant at the age of 14 and gave birth to a little person who would become the love of my life. I was fascinated by him. He was the most precious little person I had ever seen. About two and a half years later, helping to care for him became a chore. I would ask Mom if I could go across the street to the little community dances or to swim and her answer would always be, "No baby, not this time. You stay here and help me with PJ." When Doll would ask to go places, she would be allowed to most of the time. Perhaps this was because she tried her best to be trusted by mom and dad again. Maybe she regained their trust, I don't know. Doll even got to go on a two week excursion without any problems. Mom and Dad allowed Doll to go visit Evelyn and her husband on the Army base while, you guessed it, I had to stay home and help take care of my little nephew. I would get so angry. I once told Mom, "If I have to stay here and take care of everyone else's children, I may as well have one of my own." I meant that! From that point on, I became very rebellious. I would play hooky from school and just mess around all day, doing nothing. I started smoking weed and cigarettes and drinking wine.

This new found behavior seemed to lessen my adolescent cares. I would come home, filled with uncontrollable giggles and glassy red eyes. Dad was none the wiser but Mom was the wise one. I remember her just looking at me from head to toe, never saying one word. Later when I was a grown woman and asked her about those times, she replied, "I knew you were doing that ole dope."

My associates were mainly guys. I found guys to be very cool and more trustworthy than girls. They never gossiped and talked about each other and I liked that. I was not sleeping with them, just hanging out with them. They always had lots of weed to smoke too so hanging out with them was an added bonus. There was this one guy named Reggie. Reggie was very attractive, both inside and out. We grew very close in a short time. Our friendship soon turned into an intimate relationship. I really believe Reggie loved me. There was nothing he would not do for me. He was one of the kindest guys I've ever known. Reggie was very special indeed. The main problem was Mom did not like him. She took one look at him, from head to toe of course, and immediately decided that she did not want me to have anything to do with him. Thus, that whirlwind courtship/friendship was doomed from the very start.

Doll and I were riding down the street one day. We always did the grocery shopping. Dad would sign a check and give Doll the car keys. I enjoyed these shopping trips because this made it possible for me to purchase my wine, and cigarettes. I knew that Dad never checked the grocery receipts so this was a sweet deal for me. Doll was cool with me too. She never told on me. Anyway, on our way back home from the grocery store, we saw this guy that was very attractive. He was dressed in a sky blue outfit complete with a sky blue hat with a feather

sticking out of it, and sky blue, suede high heeled shoes. I immediately told Doll to turn the car around because I just had
to know who he was. I asked him for his name and gave him
my phone number. And so, the long, 12 year saga of my pre-
mature adult life was about to begin.

Chapter 4

Tyrone. That was his name. He was short in statue but talked a tall game. I was fascinated by his fast talking and adventurous tales. Of course, this man must have been sent from heaven. Since I was raised to know, without any doubts, that there was no such thing as people intentionally harming you, surely this man could not have any ill intentions where I was concerned. All my life, I had been taught that there were no wolves in sheep's clothing, and if there were, just turn the other cheek anyway. God would surely bless you all the more if you would do this. I was just 15 years old when I met Tyrone.

Boy oh boy, did I ever grow and mature at record speed after meeting him. I didn't have to wait long until he called me. I was swooning as I spoke with him, clinging to his every smooth word. We decided that he should come over to meet my family and I also wanted to see how my mom's scrutinizing eye would perceive him. We decided that he should come over on Sunday evening. Well, Sunday evening came rapidly and I had butterflies in my stomach when I heard the knock on the door. When I opened the door for Tyrone, I could have fainted at his appearance. He was dressed in a black three piece suit, black shiny shoes and a black top hat to match. Now that I think about it, he reminded me of a funeral parlor attendant. My dad was immediately taken with Tyrone. I think it was the suit with the matching accessories that did it for my dad as well. On the other hand, mom took one long, scrutinizing look at him and immediately turned her nose up in a very disapproving manner. Tyrone was the perfect date. He said all the right things to dad, mom and me and had my dad and me clinging to his every word. Mom on the other hand was not impressed one bit. After our lengthy visit, Tyrone kissed me goodbye on my cheek and I just knew I had died and gone to heaven. "What a great guy" is all I could think of. Dad was quite impressed too. Mom said, "Cheryl, I know his family and they have always had a reputation of being sorry and no good for the most part. The men, especially his uncle, have gotten more women pregnant than a little bit. He's as sorry as the rest of the ones that I know." Well, I surely knew right then that mom had definitely bumped her head. She was the most hard-nosed, delusional woman that I had ever known, ever. Despite whatever picture there was in my mom's mind, Tyrone and I continued to date. I remember seeing Reggie on an occasion after I broke up with him. I'll never forget what he told me; "Baby, he's bad for you, he'll hurt you", meaning of course, Tyrone. I want to thank you right here and now Reggie for caring enough to tell me that, thank you so much.

Tyrone and I continued to see each other and my mom continued to protest. Dad continued to be as taken with Tyrone as I was so Tyrone was allowed to continue his visits to our home. Mom and Dad still would not allow me to go out on a date with Tyrone so our visits were restricted to the house. As time went by, I found myself wanting to give this wonderfully intriguing man the most prized possession I feel anyone has, themselves sexually. Tyrone and I came up with a plan; Tyrone always had the world's best plans. We decided that I would sneak him upstairs in my bedroom when my parents went to sleep. That is exactly what we did. As soon as I heard the ole familiar signs of definite sleep from my parent's bedroom, very loud snoring that seemed to compliment each other; I opened the hallway door and beckoned for Tyrone to come inside. He removed his shoes so as not to make any excess noise while tiptoeing up to my room. The lock on my bedroom door was broken so we propped a board against it and the bottom of the bed to substitute for a lock. We sat on the bed and smoked weed and drank some of a bottle of wine, compliments of Bishop John, indirectly of course. Tyrone lifted the window so that the weed scent could go outside. After we were giggling and very tipsy, we started kissing. One thing led to another and before long, we were completely naked and engaging in sex. All of a sudden, mom was coming up the stairs. She was banging on the door and demanding that I open it. I was frozen stiff and, needless to say, my high was blown. I didn't know what to do. Tyrone was afraid too. He always knew the right things to say but now, he was still and quiet as a mute button. Then, suddenly he jumped up and when he did, he knocked the stick down from the door. My mom came bursting in the room. She was hysterical. She said, "Cheryl, where are your clothes?" I was scared to the point of not responding to her question. Then, she looked across the room where Tyrone was standing there, stark naked, clothes in hand. Mom immediately went over to him and started hitting him. Tyrone rushed to the opened window and jumped out of it and down two stories to the ground. All of this commotion had awakened dad.

As he was making his way upstairs, my mom threw me my clothes and ordered for me to get dressed. I quickly complied. When dad was in my bedroom, mom hurriedly told him what had just happened. I just stood there looking very stupid. Dad was absolutely furious! He hauled us all in the car and took us straight to the police department. There, my parents filed a warrant against Tyrone.

Chapter 5

Our house was very quiet and tense. The tension was so thick; I think one could have actually cut it with a knife. I was very nervous about going to court and I was also very sad that Tyrone had been forbidden to come to see me again. When the big court date finally arrived, there it was made legal. I could not have anything more to do with Tyrone and he could never bother me again. I knew I was in love with him, even at 15, and I didn't want to live if I couldn't see him. After this court thing was all over, I went home and tried to think what the best course of action was for me to take now. I was in the 11th grade in school. Even though I was very smart, I didn't put my best effort into my school work because all I could think of was Tyrone. Tyrone said he missed me as much as I missed him and all I could think of was, "How could my mom and dad be so cruel as to destroy something as beautiful as what Tyrone and I have together?" Tyrone's thinking cap was definitely intact once again. He encouraged me to play hooky from school and it sounded like a pretty good idea to me. So that is how we started to see each other again. If I didn't or couldn't leave school early due to a test or an exam, I would finish the day out in school only to come home and hide in the attic from my mom. I would hear her downstairs and in my room calling me and looking for me. I would remain very quiet until I heard that ole familiar sound of her car motor and soon I would see her driving slowly down the street. She would be going to look for me. Now, as I sit here reflecting back on that, I feel really bad about hurting my mother at all. I took advantage of her hearing deficit by hiding in the house or talking quietly on the telephone to Tyrone, knowing full well mom couldn't hear me. Anyway, when she would leave to look for me, I'd bathe, change clothes, get more clothes to wear to school for the next day and leave to meet Tyrone. There was this vacant house just down the street from our house. Tyrone said he was taking care of the house for the owners, but later I found out that he really wasn't. It was a beautiful house and very comfortable. That was our hangout. A lot of days, we'd be lying around that house, smoking weed and having sex. Sometimes, I would be looking through the window and see my mother walking down the street carrying her favorite stick, looking very troubled and I would begin to feel very bad. Ole Tyrone would soon be talking that talk that knocked me off of my feet and reassuring me that we were doing the right thing since we'd been forbidden to see each other any other way. Then, I'd settle back down to what we were doing; settle back into this comfortable love affair that was surely made in heaven. Eventually, I felt so bad for mom and I went back home. One early spring morning, dad, mom and I were sitting down to breakfast. My mom was so quietly intuitive that sometimes it was scary. What really got next to me was the way she could give you that once over from head to toe, then come back up to look you square in the eyes. Anyway, mom had prepared bacon and oatmeal. The oatmeal was very tasty but midway through it I felt so nauseated. Mom just sat there with "that look" as I took deep breaths trying to keep that oatmeal down. I abruptly excused myself from the table and after I threw up what seemed like a whole pot of oatmeal, there was mom, standing there in the hallway scowling at me. After I resumed some sort of composure, mom simply stated, "You're pregnant." Well, that was certainly news to me! As with everything else, mom was right. I was pregnant, about 2 months. I abruptly ran away again.

This behavior went on and on and finally one day, my dad cornered me walking down the street. I would always run from my mom when she tried to get me to talk to her, but with my dad, I would stop and talk to him. He told me to get inside the car and talk with him on this particular day; I did. He said, "Cheryl, we're going to let you go. If this is what you want or what you think you want, and clearly, that seems to be the case, we're going to let you. Meet us down at the police station and we'll have you liberated." Well, I didn't know what to think or say or do for that matter. My parents never lied to me so I knew that he was serious. I'll never forget going to that little police station. Tyrone walked me down to the station but he said that they wanted to see me, not him, so he waited outside for me, out of clear sight of everyone. There, mom and dad were sitting looking at me as the police officer labeled me as an incorrigible teenager and gave me my freedom from my parents at the tender age of 16. My mom was crying and she told me, "You look hungry." She gave me a couple of her little wrinkled dollar bills and told me to get myself something to eat. I will never, ever forget that encounter with my mom that day. It breaks my heart even to this day. When this process was completed my dad said, "Cheryl, do you see those big beautiful eyes you have?" I just simply nodded. He went on to say, "They're going to cry and cry and cry." That was the legacy my dad left with me that day. I managed to graduate at the age of 16. It was always easy for me to learn anything rather quickly, so breezing through 12th grade a year early was no different. Dad was there to see me walk across the stage, three months pregnant and all, but mom was nowhere to be found. She was so disappointed in me and with all the unfavorable choices I was making. I couldn't see what the big deal was, not then anyway.

Chapter 6

It was a very long, very hot summer. I was living with Martha and Jake, Tyrone's mom and stepfather. Even though I appreciated Martha's generosity of allowing Tyrone and I to stay with her, the adjustment was quite a culture shock and that's putting it mildly. My dad worked hard to make a very comfortable life for us. His wife and children wore the finest of clothing. There were always lots of great foods to eat, all electric appliances, and indoor plumbing. Martha loved to cook and she was an excellent cook but there was one catch; she cooked on a wood stove. She also washed on a wringer type washing machine and since she had no dryer, it was hanging the clothes out on the clothes line or going to the laundromat. Martha always cooked three meals daily and even though the food was very tasty, I often feared that I would fall out from heat exhaustion or worse, have a heat stroke right there in the middle of her kitchen. We would all be eating and sweating. Since there was no running water, almost after every meal, the nausea from my pregnancy overtook me. I found myself running out of the back door and down through the back yard to the outdoor toilet. I remember being so afraid to lean my head over the wooden seat of that toilet. I just knew that in the midst of throwing up, a snake would slither right out from that wooden toilet seat and crawl right down my throat as I leaned there heaving my guts out. I had this same nightmarish fear when I had to sit down on that seat and it seemed that I always had to pee nonstop. At night, I had my times with the good ole "slop jar." Whoever named it surely gave it the right name. It was a sloppy process indeed. I had never ever seen, nor heard of a cockroach until I stayed with Martha and Jake. There seemed to be millions of these little brown, smelly creatures running around as well. Yes, living with them was a culture shock indeed. It was better than being outside though and besides, I loved myself some Tyrone. I had grown very close to Martha too. She did everything she could for me and she was there for me in a very difficult time in my life. I'll always thank and appreciate her for that. I liked Jake too. He was a quiet man for the most part but it was said that if anyone messed with him, he would shoot them right there on the spot. He was a very unusual man as well. He could not read or write and he was afraid of doll babies and Halloween costumes. On Halloween, all of the children knew not to come to his house. He dipped snuff and Martha smoked Salem 100's. I remember them sitting on the front porch on summer evenings. Jake would be sitting in his chair with his spit can beside him. Martha would sit in her swing with her cigarette hanging from her mouth with the ashes longer than the cigarette. The ashes never fell and I've always wondered how she accomplished that. Martha loved to play a card game called deuces wild. Their whole family did. If Martha wasn't playing on her front porch, she was playing in her house or one of her aunt's houses or friend's houses. That cigarette would be hanging from her mouth with those long ashes intact as she argued and made up new rules when she was losing and was happy as all get out when she wasn't.

Mom still did not care for Tyrone or Martha. She would drive down the street and park beside Martha's house and blow the horn for me to come out. I'd be so glad to see her. When I'd get inside the car to sit and talk with her, she would hand me a few dollars, some fruits and juices. After all I had put her through she still loved me. Surely, a mother's love is second only to God's.

Around early fall, Tyrone found a real job doing maintenance in the school system. We moved to his uncle's house which had electric but no running water, but what did that matter? By now, I was a pro at running back and forth to the outhouse and emptying the slop jar in the mornings. Tyrone didn't see much need in having groceries in our little house so we continued to eat our meals at Martha's house. I never questioned Tyrone because I was raised to know that the man was indeed the head of his household. Tyrone's ideas of taking care of his household were a far cry from what I had been accustomed to all of my life though, but still I never questioned it. I did learn how to be patiently hungry until Martha was ready to serve meals though. Often mom would come by with sacks of foods, fruits, vegetables, juices and I was so glad to see her. She would never come inside; she would just honk the horn until I came out to meet her. I cannot, to this day tell you how moved I was to see that mom still loved me despite her total disappointment in me.

I received an acceptance letter to attend nursing school in September but, as fate would have it, I didn't have the money. I felt reasonably sure that Tyrone wouldn't finance school either so I didn't even bother asking him. It was a struggle to even eat proper meals because Tyrone never saw the importance of going to the grocery store. So, regretfully, I sat school out. Besides, I was very pregnant and feeling pretty lousy most of the time, at least, that is the excuse I used to comfort myself anyway.

One late fall morning, dad came over to the house. He said he needed to talk with us. This was his first visit to my new "humble abode" so I was quite shocked to see him. He blew for me to come out and as usual, I complied. He said, "Cheryl, you are living in sin, over here shacking up with this man. If you two love each other and intend to continue to live together, you need to get married." Well, Tyrone heard this too so we decided to get married. I was so excited that Tyrone agreed to this latest arrangement. I loved him with all my heart and I knew that I wanted to spend the rest of my life with him. We set the wedding date for November 20th. We completed the preliminary requirement which was to go to the doctor to get our blood tested. On the morning of November 20th, I awoke early. I couldn't sleep because I was so very excited. Tyrone did not wake early with me. I waited and waited for what seemed hours. Finally, I could not contain my excitement any longer. I said, "Tyrone, wake up. We have to go to the clerk's office to get our marriage license before it closes. You know today is our big day!" His response to that was a very hard, sharp slap to my face. I was stunned. I don't know which hurt worse, the slap or my feelings at that moment. After striking me he says, "I'm going to get the damned license, don't rush me." I wasn't quite sure what to say or do. It seemed the only thing left for me to do was to go in the next room, sit quietly in a corner, and cry what seemed like a river of tears. This was the first time that Tyrone ever put his hands on me to hurt me but, as it turned out, not the last.

Chapter 7

Tyrone vowed never to hit me again. He was his ole self again, that loving, sweet talking man that I fell in love with. I believed him when he said he was just nervous and that I shocked him by waking him up so abruptly. Of course, I forgave him instantly. After all, wasn't this the way I had been taught all of my life, to turn the other cheek?

On our wedding day, I wore the maternity dress that mom bought for me about 2 months earlier. It was the only good dress I now owned. My shoes were not that good. They had a lot of wear and tear but they were all I had so they were what I wore. Tyrone, of course was cleaner than the board of health. He always was. I guess he didn't see the need to spend perfectly good money on maternity clothes for me. After all, I wasn't going to be pregnant forever was I? We were married at Orlando's house. He and my dear sister-n-law, Mae, lived right around the corner from Tyrone and me. Martha was present, her daughter Queeta, and a couple of Tyrone's aunts were also present. But my dear mother's presence was, yet again, sorely missed. She had not been in favor of any relationship with

Tyrone and she remained unmoved. Dear ole dad married us. I'm not sure what emotions were flowing throughout my body that night, mixed I suppose. Tyrone didn't look the slightest bit happy but I chalked it up to him just being nervous. I knew that I had made poor choices before and now I would at least make my dad proud of, firstly, not "living in sin any longer" and secondly, allowing him to marry his baby girl. Neither one of us had a ring to show our unending love and commitment to each other, and after the ceremony, we walked home in silence. Tyrone just sat on the sofa quietly all that night. I lay in bed alone, feeling very alone. The only consolation I felt that night was my unborn child kicking inside me as if to tell me, "Mama, everything's going to be alright." It felt more like we were just coming from a funeral instead of our wedding.

Weeks passed and I became heavier and heavier with our unborn child. My due date was December 17th. It got to be December 30th and still no baby. Dr. Traylor, who had been my next door neighbor for years, called me into his office on December 30th. He said, "Cheryl, you're not ever going to have that baby are you?" These were my exact sentiments! I just knew I'd be pregnant forever. Dr. Traylor must have seen the look of utter despair on my face because he said, "I want you to go to the drug store and buy a bottle of castor oil. I want you to drink the entire four ounces. With any luck, you'll be able to claim this baby on your tax return for the year." I didn't see the humor in this situation that he obviously did but I decided to try this remedy anyway. After all, what could it hurt? So, I went over to my mom's house to tell her of the advice I'd just been given. Mom gave me the money for the castor oil and took me to purchase it.

My dear sister Evelyn was home on leave from the Army. Having her with me was very comforting. We were all sitting around in the living room of my mother's house. I was sitting there very nervous. I wasn't really feeling any major discomfort other than those pains you feel from drinking 4 ounces of castor oil. I seemed to have to run to the bathroom every 15 minutes! I think Tyrone was over Mom's house that evening but I'm not sure. As the evening grew, I begin to feel kind of cramp like pains in my stomach and back. Mom and Evelyn thought it was time for me to go to the hospital. I was very, very nervous by this time because I had no idea what to expect, but I hadn't heard any good things about labor up to this point, only that it HURT! So, Dad loaded me in his car and Mom, Evelyn and I were in route to the hospital. Just as soon as we entered the emergency room I remember the nurse wheeling me around to the labor and delivery department. I was placed in a room and given a gown and instructed to lie down in bed. I was then placed on a monitor and I could hear my baby's heartbeat strong and healthy. "That right there is worth all the pain that I'm feeling right now," I thought to myself as I listened. As the evening grew into night, my pains were becoming unbearable seemingly. I remember only having maybe a couple minutes of recovery before the next stretch of a contraction would ripple through my body. Just when I knew I could take no more, I was pulled down to the foot of this steel-looking table with my feet placed in stirrups, and being asked to "push down" as hard as I could! Tyrone was in there with me and I could tell he was as nervous as he could be. Anyway, I was pushing with each contraction with all of my might. I just wanted this pain to stop. I am convinced that there is no pain greater in this world than that of child birth. I could be wrong. I remember Dr. Traylor cutting my bottom. I saw this long needle and I know he stuck it in me but I was in so much pain, it really didn't matter at this point. Then I was asked to push really hard; I did. Suddenly, Dr. Traylor says, "don't push, just breath. There was something bobbing between my legs with a mound of hair on it, but there was no other body part showing!! Then Dr. Traylor says, "Push, push hard." It felt like the biggest relief in my whole lifetime. The baby was out and Dr. Traylor was saying, "It's a boy, it's a boy" and what a beautiful boy he was. Oh my God, was all I could think. What a great New Year's gift!

Tyrone Jr. That was what we decided to name him. Tyrone was strutting around the place just as proud as a peacock. The fact that everyone kept on telling Tyrone that "that baby looks just like you" made him feel even that much more proud. Tyrone Jr. was a true little blessing. It was true. He did look just like his father. He had the prettiest head of black straight hair and he was just adorable. He was perfectly healthy. He was born with two extra fingers and two extra toes. This trait, I found out, came from Tyrone's side of the family. At any rate, it only took tying them off with black thread to resolve that little issue.

When it came time for us to leave the hospital, Mom and Evelyn thought it would be better if the baby and I stayed over Mom's until I was up and around again. Considering I had to have stitches and looked like Herman the Munster when I walked, I thought it was a terrific idea. Besides, the house where Tyrone and I stayed was not adequate heat wise and I couldn't even cook meals there. I really didn't feel like dealing with waiting for Martha to get home before I could eat, keeping a wood fire going or any of that stuff now. Staying with mom, dad and having Evelyn there was very comfortable and enjoyable. I knew I was around family and I knew that they loved me, no matter what. I was spoiled and honestly, I needed a little spoiling. I'd forgotten what that felt like lately.

Regular meals were prepared for me and I thoroughly enjoyed them. I would watch in total fascination as Mom would be bathing little Tyrone as he'd be squalling like someone was trying to kill him. She'd just be talking to him and flipping him over like a little flapjack. Mom refused to call the baby Tyrone because she really didn't like big Tyrone at all. She said, "I'm going to call him ManBoy" to which I said to myself, "Oh, no you're not." Tyrone Sr. would come over to visit us and when he did, I always sensed his feeling very much out of place. He used to love to sit there holding the baby and brushing his hair, brushing it in different little styles. I thought, "This might just turn out all right anyway. I know I sure do love him at this moment."

Chapter 8

Tyrone decided to nickname the baby himself. It seemed that almost all of his family had nicknames. That was a very odd conception for me because until now, I never even knew anyone by anything other than their birth names, now here I was watching as my mom and Tyrone were trying to decide a nickname for my baby. Boobie is the name that Tyrone came up with so we all started calling him that, even mom. I called him "My little Poopa" for a long time.

It had been two weeks and although I was nowhere near ready to move back into "my humble abode" I had to leave. I was blessed with so many wonderful baby clothes and shoes for Boobie so I didn't have that to worry about. I was a little concerned about the formula but I had faith that God would work that out too. Shortly after returning home, Tyrone's uncle needed to move back into his house so we were forced to move. Tyrone found this nice man, Mr. Pete, who said we could live with him and pay forty dollars a month for a room. The house was a small house but it was better than being outside. We again had a wood stove and a hotplate so

I could keep Boobie warm and cook something to eat. I was pleased with this. There was also a telephone in our room. A telephone that I never even thought twice about as a child growing up at home was now a luxury. We could store food items in Mr. Pete's refrigerator too. There was not much food to worry about storing because Tyrone basically never bought a lot of groceries. I honestly don't ever remember him going to the grocery store with a grocery list as I was so accustomed to doing before this drastic lifestyle change. On the rare occasions that Tyrone would call home to check on me, I would say to him, "Tyrone, I'm hungry. I need something to eat." He would reply, "I already ate at work." I often wondered how he thought his full stomach was supposed to fill my empty one. There were a lot of days when I didn't have anything to eat. I remember once, I was so hungry I would eat Boobie's baby aspirin. I was afraid to say anything to my parents because I didn't want to hear "I told you so." Formula for Boobie was becoming a problem too. I remember walking to the shopping center with Boobie in one arm, and diaper bag in the other arm. I would go to this little drug store that was located in the shopping mall and fill the diaper bag up with formula. I'm almost certain the employees there knew I was stealing formula but no one ever said anything. I would feel really condemned about stealing and I vowed to stop it. What would really make me so angry would be Tyrone coming home and actually drinking the formula and eating Boobie's baby deserts. This would boil my blood! I could hardly keep formula and foods for the baby because the daddy liked it as much or more than the baby did.

One day, I was on one of my routine trips to the drug store. I mustered up enough nerve to ask the manager if I could open up a charge account so that I could purchase formula and other much needed supplies for Boobie. To my surprise and gratefulness, he said yes. I could only cry tears of joy and relief. I told Tyrone of our new charge account when he came home that afternoon and he said, "Good Cheryl, now who's going to pay for it? I was very amazed that this man had no desire to feed me or his baby. All the sweet, thoughtful things Tyrone used to say to me were no more. This was a different man entirely. What happened to that sweet Tyrone that I knew not so long ago? Tyrone would leave for work early in the mornings and he would come home very late at night, if he came home at all. He would cut enough wood to last for about a week so that we would not be cold and I do thank him for that. On a good day, he would come home from work with food and every now and then, he would actually cook for us. He would be sweet every now and then but these nice episodes were sporadic and few and far between.

I wouldn't go anywhere during the long days and they would slowly turn into weeks where I would be inside the house. I didn't have adequate clothes and I was ashamed to be seen if I didn't have to. I was ashamed that I left my father's home to be with a man who obviously didn't feel as strongly about me as I did him. My eating habits were so inconsistent that I actually lost a lot of weight. I was weighing 125 pounds but that was slowly dwindling away. I finally broke down one day and went to my parent's home. I told them I was hungry and Tyrone was not being a good provider at all. Mom was very hurt by this. She started to fix me a plate of food when Dad said, "That is your problem, it is not our problem. You take your problem, meaning Boobie, and you go back to your house because you are Tyrone's responsibility now." I was so stunned, I wasn't sure I heard Dad correctly. I was sure when he refused to let Mom give me the food. When Dad left the room, Mom told me to go upstairs and she actually sneaked me a plate of food upstairs. This sneaking food went on for some time. I could not understand how Dad could preach to a church full of people about God's love for us and how we should love one another, yet turn his daughter and grandson away. I was perplexed with this for a long time. I was so tired of having Mom sneak me upstairs and bring me food. This was very, very old. It was not until I lost down to 96 pounds and begin to have an ashen look to my complexion that Dad invited me to eat freely from his table. He never missed an opportunity to tell people about how he had to feed me and my "problem" because I didn't have a husband who would take care of his responsibilities. I remember on holidays when all of my sisters and brothers and their families would come home, Dad never missed the opportunity to say "Cheryl was about to starve to death around here, looking like walking death until I took her and Boobie in and fed them." How embarrassing this would be but I would simply lower my head to keep from making eye contact with anyone. Although I was grateful for Dad feeding us, I was always apprehensive about eating with them. I felt bad enough having to lay what little pride I had aside and even admit to being hungry in the first place. Dad certainly didn't make me feel any better.

I never knew about any kind of public assistance because I had never been in a position where I needed to know about food stamps and stuff before. I remember talking to this girl one day while walking from Mom's house. Her name was Sheila. She was a nice girl who had been going through a lot of bad times herself. She told me about how she got food stamps for her and her child and even a check once a month because her man was "locked up." I thanked her for the information and immediately made an appointment at the Department of

Social Services. On the day of my appointment, I was astonished to know that I would be getting food stamps, more than enough to feed my little family and that they would be retroactive as well. I had to wait for them to be mailed though. I was beside myself with joy and thanksgiving.

On the day that the food stamps arrived, I asked Dad to take me to the grocery store. He did. I had about two-hundred dollars in food stamps and I spent everything except about twenty-dollars. I told Dad that since he was so good to let me eat from his table, this grocery was for him and Mom. He was a very happy man, let me tell you. So, after this massive grocery shopping, Dad took me back to his house where I unloaded all of the groceries in his cabinets, refrigerator and freezer. I've always been the kind of person that had a very sincere and giving heart and I was glad to repay Dad in the only form I could. As I walked back to my little room of a home, I felt sad that I hadn't bought any food for us, but I was happy to feel that I had paid Dad for his pity for me in some small way. As time went on and I received food stamps, Tyrone would accompany me to the grocery store. He would walk around the store with me, loading the basket with all the things that he wanted. He had this other weird thing he did too. He would sometimes be dressed as a military person and as we were walking around in the store, as we approached people, he would start speaking with a foreign accent. He'd say things like, "Cheryl, we must hurry because my flight leaves in a couple hours. I can't be late because I must be in France by tomorrow." Talk about delusions of grandeur. He had a major case of it. As soon as we would get to the check out, he immediately thought of some urgent emergency that he had to do outside. When I would pay for the grocery with the food stamps, he would show up at the curb outside to help me put the food in the car. It was as if Tyrone was ashamed of our blessing; food, and food stamps!

I don't know whether Tyrone didn't pay Mr. Pete or just what the circumstance was but we again had to move. There was this house on the corner of the street from Mr. Pete's house and we were able to move there. It could have been a nice little place but Tyrone did not pay bills in a timely manner, so most of the time, our water was turned off and sometimes even our electricity was off as well. There was a living room, kitchen and bathroom downstairs and two bedrooms upstairs. We kept the downstairs sealed off from the upstairs because we only had one wood heater and that was in the upstairs bedroom. Tyrone never thought to buy another wood heater for the downstairs area I suppose. I would continue to supply Dad's house with the food purchased with the food stamps because a lot of the time I really didn't have anywhere to store it anyway.

I was so tired of living like this. I knew that I had more potential than just to sit in the house all day. I also knew that most days I wouldn't see Tyrone until late at night or in a day or so. Sometimes I would be so depressed until I would just sit and cry and cry. Dad had been my best friend when I was a little girl and sometimes I found it easy to talk to him even now. He always knew just how to put things in proper perspective. I remember being so down and feeling like God, if He existed, didn't like me very much. One day I asked, "Dad, how do I even know that there is a God?" He smiled as he led me to the breakfast room window. He asked, "Cheryl, do you see those trees out there?" I simply nodded. Then he went on to ask, "Do you see the leaves blowing on the trees?" Again, I nodded. He then asked, "What is causing those leaves to blow?" I thought this was a very odd question but I immediately said,

"The wind Dad." He then asked, "How do you know it's the wind, can you see the wind?" I acknowledged that no I could not see the wind. He went on to explain to me, "That's how we know there is a God. We cannot see Him but we can see the effects of His mighty works. That is where faith comes in. Even though we cannot see a thing, by having faith, we know that the unseen exists." This made perfect sense to me and I never questioned God's existence again.

I decided to go out job hunting. I asked Mom if she would keep Boobie for me while I worked and of course she said she would. Dad again was not happy with this arrangement. He kept going on and on about "You're taking my wife from me. This is the time of our lives when we should be enjoying each other, not worrying with a baby." But Dad, I would argue, Boobie is such a good baby. He rarely even cries for anything. Much to Dad's dismay, Mom firmly said she would keep Boobie and that was that. I found a job at Pizza Hut as a waitress. I loved the job, my coworkers, the customers and my tips. I felt that I would really achieve some goals now. I needed a car and I found a nice little stick shift. Mom cosigned for me and I bought the car. After much going around town stopping in the middle of traffic and stalling out at a stop light, I finally got the hang of driving a stick. It was actually fun after a while. I'm still quite surprised that I didn't get whiplash while learning though.

Tyrone was happy about the car too. He had such a bad temper most of the time. It seemed the least little thing I did would require him to jump on me and physically beat me, only to later make up to me by having sex with me. He wanted to take me to work everyday and keep my car. I was afraid to tell him no because I didn't want to spark his temper. So, this went on for some time. He would drop me off and pick me up everyday. I would find cigarette butts with lipstick on them in the ashtray and when I'd ask about it, he would simply say, "I gave this little lady a ride because she was carrying a lot of bags." I would let it drop but I didn't believe him for a second.

I was starting to feel pretty good about myself again and my self-esteem began to slowly blossom. I was making great tips because I loved what I did and I'd always loved to serve and wait on others. That always made me happy; feeling that I was doing something to make others happy. I always kept all my tips for the day in a pocketbook. One morning, I remember lying in bed. I wasn't asleep but Tyrone thought I was. I watched as he went into my pocketbook and took some of my tip money, all the while watching me to see if I were asleep. I never said anything to him about it and he doesn't know that I know he was stealing my money to this day. I decided to save my tips in a more secure place because I decided to open a saving's account for Boobie. I saved a grand total of seventy-five dollars and I was quite proud of this accomplishment. I carefully placed the coins in wrappers before going to work the next morning. Since I had to go to work and since I knew I would not have the luxury of keeping my car, I asked Tyrone if he would go to the bank and open a savings account for Boobie. He gladly said that he would. Later that evening I was finished working. I stood outside waiting for Tyrone to pick me up. I waited and waited but he never came. I was very angry and I decided to walk, thinking that perhaps I would see him. When I approached that same little shopping center that, not so long ago, I would go to steal formula for Boobie, I saw Tyrone in the car. There was a lady with him. I knew this lady because of the very small town we lived in. Her name was Bev. There were all kinds of packages in the back seat of the car. As I approached them, he pulled off. Later, when he did come home, he came in very angry. He would always come home like this, especially when he had done something and I found out about it, or he wanted an excuse to go back out as soon as he came in. I said, "Tyrone, didn't you see me today walking to the car? Why did you pull off and why did I have to walk home in the first place? Where is the money for the savings account? Did you even open it? Well, this interrogation made him mad. He slapped me and pushed me down as he proceeded to beat me. As he was beating me he was saying, "You don't ever trust me to do anything right. You're always accusing me of other women and I'm tired of it." I was afraid to fight back. I never wanted to hurt him because I loved him so much. He surely found it very easy to hurt me though. After his tantrum was over, he left out of the room, slammed the back door behind him and sped off in my car. I was so hurt; I cannot find the words to express how much even now. There went all of my hard earned tips and self-esteem with it. Tyrone to this day, has never mentioned spending our baby's money on some tramp of a woman.

Chapter 9

I was upset most of the time. I would go over and talk to Dad and get advice from him. "Dad, I'm so tired of living with Tyrone but I don't have anywhere to go. I feel trapped. I love him but I don't feel that he loves me." Dad would always say, "Cheryl, you married this man for better or for worse. I know because I married you myself. Just do God's will and always remember, a sanctified wife sanctifies her husband." So, I stayed with him mostly for those reasons. Then too, I did love him.

After every beating, Tyrone would come back and bring me little gifts. They would be those little sun dresses that were very straight and plain and had elastic in the front. They were very shapeless dresses. Tyrone was extremely jealous and did not want me to dress where much of my body would show. I was a very shapely woman and he did not want anyone else to be attracted to me I suppose. He was ridiculously jealous; I don't really know just how to define it. Anyway, whenever his friends would come over to see him, he would always ask me to go in the back of the house or somewhere out of sight. I thought this was utterly ridiculous but to avoid any fighting, I complied. Now, thinking back on it, Tyrone might not have wanted anyone else to know he was married, except for me that is. We would always make up after every fight and he would actually be the ole Tyrone I used to know, at least for a couple of weeks anyway. Then it would get back to being the same ole thing. I remembered my Dad's words of advice and continued to try to be that virtuous wife that would someday transform her husband into a man of the cloth or something nice.

In October of that year, I found out that I was pregnant. Normally, I should have been ecstatic, but I was not. I did not use birth control because here again, I was taught that "God knows how many children or whatever else you need, you don't have to figure His work out for Him." So here I was, very pregnant and very unhappy. Tyrone said, "I told you I only wanted one baby so have an abortion if you want to." I knew that I would never have an abortion so that was not an option. Instead, I went through, mostly alone again, almost ten months of a very unhappy pregnancy. In July, our baby girl was born. What a beautiful sight she was. I knew right then why I could have never had an abortion. I named her Cherylyn so that she would have a portion of my name. Tyrone put the middle name in there. He didn't seem too pleased to have a daughter and I felt he always favored Boobie over Cherylyn. Cherylyn was a very fussy baby. Nothing would seem to soothe her, not even taking her for long rides. She would cry all the way from home and back home. I attributed her mood to my pregnancy. I cried most of my pregnancy. Nonetheless, I loved her with all of my heart and I was very proud to have her. I was not working now so I had all the time to devote to being a loving mother, and I did. Not much had changed with Tyrone and me. I stayed at home all day, everyday, and he would go to work and come home whenever he felt like it. Our water would get turned off here and there, but somehow I managed. There was this very sweet little lady that lived next door to us. She would let me have water from her house when ours was off and to this day, I'll never forget her kindness.

It was four weeks after I had Cherylyn that Tyrone insisted on having sex with me. I told him, "Dr. Traylor said I should wait six weeks Tyrone, not four." He was not hearing that. I gave in to Tyrone that night. About three weeks later, I was having the worst pains in my stomach. I was actually bent over with the pain. I had a horrible vaginal discharge as well. I went to the doctor and he immediately sent me over to the hospital to be admitted. I was dumbfounded. I had absolutely no clue. Once there, after settling down in my hospital room, an IV was started on me. The doctor came in and told me I had gonor-rhea. Dr. Walton was a very sweet doctor but he had a hearing deficit so he said it extremely loud. I was absolutely floored. I was so upset until I could not be still. I remember thrashing around in that bed until a nurse came in and gave me a shot of something through my IV line. I don't know what it was but I went to sleep for what seemed like hours. When I awoke, another very sweet nurse came in. She knew Tyrone because he had stopped working for the school board and found a job working as an orderly there at the hospital. Anyway, she came in with her very sweet bedside manner. She said, "You should leave Tyrone. I would not stay with any man who brought a disease home to me. He's not worth it." Later, when Tyrone peeked his head in my hospital room, I asked him to come in. I said, "Tyrone, if you knew you had gonorrhea, why on earth did you give it to me?" Tyrone was always the expert at ex-plaining away his shortcomings. He said, "Cheryl, you didn't get that from me. I think you got it from sitting on a dirty toilet seat." I knew I didn't have that much medical knowledge but I certainly knew that was not true. For the life of me, I don't know why I didn't leave him right then and there, but I didn't.

After my hospital stay, I went back home. I was afraid to let Tyrone touch me. I was very unhappy with him and I didn't trust him at all. I told my sister Doll about what happened and she suggested that I come to Philadelphia to live with her. In the winter of that year, I decided that I would take her up on the offer. I remember going to Philadelphia on the Trailways bus. All I had were a few personal belongings, a little bit of money and my two babies. I cannot tell you how alone and totally helpless I felt at that moment. I remember this nice little old lady sitting behind me. I had been crying and rocking Cherylyn in my arms and soothing Boobie in the seat next to me. I hadn't noticed the lady watching me. Finally she said, "You poor, poor dear." Well, the tears really began to fall then. I was having a pity party out of this world! The little old lady just sat quietly behind me and rubbed my shoulders.

Philadelphia was COLD! Doll lived in a very nice home and for the most part, I enjoyed being with her. She had just had a baby a couple of months before Cherylyn was born so I stayed home and kept her baby and mine. Doll was in an abusive marriage herself and I hated to see her husband fight her like Tyrone did me. I was helpless to defend her as I'd done in childhood. I couldn't even defend myself. My spirit was totally broken. I missed my Mom and yes, for whatever reason, I missed Tyrone too. I know I should have stayed in Philadelphia but I was homesick with a vengeance. I had never been out of my little small town before and this was totally different from what I was accustomed to. Tyrone would call to say that he missed me so much. He'd say, "Cheryl, I miss you and the kids. If you'll come back home, I promise never to hit you or be mean to you again." He even made the trip up to see us once. I was convinced that he was sorry for what he had put me through so I decided, after a few months, to go back home to be with Tyrone. After all, didn't a sanctified wife sanctify her husband? Before making the trip back home, Doll took me downtown and bought me a full line of much needed clothing. She bought me everything from underwear to outfits and shoes. She always smelled great and she purchased for me wonderful perfumes and colognes too. She really treated me great and she has continued to give me and buy me lovely clothing, even to this day. I will always love and appreciate her for those acts of kindness. I went back home with a new appearance and a fresh outlook on my life. I was glad to be back with Tyrone. I was proud of my new appearance with all of my "bad rags" and heavenly smelling fragrances. No one could tell me I wasn't the foxiest woman in that small town! I was also glad to be back with my Mom. In a few short years, we had become best friends again.

Chapter 10

So here I was, right back where I started. We were forced to leave the little house on the corner for whatever reason. I learned to just listen to Tyrone's explanations, never even expecting the real reasons from him. Anyway, Tyrone hooked up with this prominent business man who ran a motel. We were given a couple of rooms at this motel which was on the very end side away from the mainstream of the motel. There were two rooms in our new house, two bedrooms to be exact, and of course, a bathroom. I was back to cooking on a hot plate again. I didn't have a job so I was again forced to totally depend on Tyrone. I was again hungry, only this time, I had two more mouths to feed. There was this little Tastee Freeze type place about two miles down the highway. Tyrone still found it necessary to take the car, thus leaving me with two babies at a motel on the highway and no transportation. Tyrone had a deal with Mr. Grey to run the motel for him, in exchange for living there free of charge. So Tyrone rented out rooms and kept the change he emptied from the vending machines. What a sweet deal this was for Tyrone. Although he was working and we were staying here free of charge, Tyrone still was no better of a provider than he ever had been. There were times when I would be so hungry again. I refused to go back to Mom and Dad. Instead, I can remember taking the keys to the vending machines, emptying the change and walking down the highway to that little Tastee Freeze type place. I would instruct Boobie to stay inside and be very quiet and watch his baby sister until I returned. I would always make sure to tell Boobie that "Mommy will be right back so don't be afraid, okay?" Boobie was always such a nice, mild mannered child. When I'd come back with hotdogs, hamburgers and whatever the change would buy, I'd find him sitting right where I left him, watching his sister. I would then feed them until I was sure they were full, and then I would eat whatever was left over. This went on for a little while. Soon, I was back at Mom's door asking her to please watch the children so I could work. I don't know what I would have done without my Mom because she never refused to help me.

I went back to the Pizza Hut and worked for a while. I could immediately tell a difference in my economics. Tyrone kept the car most of the times even though the motel was about 6 miles from town. He knew that mom would come and get me if I needed her to so he depended on that. This particular day, mom brought me home from work. Mom had both the children with her as well. When I went inside the motel room, there on the bed was my nightgown. The bed was a mess; there were blood spots on the sheets. Someone had been in my perfume as well. I brought the children inside and walked up to the office. There was Tyrone with a girl that I had known all my life. We were raised up in the same church for Pete's sake. She had her little girl with her. I immediately confronted Tyrone. He went into a rage and as I was walking back to our motel room, he ran up behind me and threw me on the ground outside the door. He then began to bang my head on the cement sidewalk. He beat me up really bad that evening. I had migraines for a lot of years after that. I always wondered if the migraines stemmed from Tyrone banging my head against the cement that day or was it Tyrone himself. Later that week, Tyrone came home with two sundresses.

Even though I was blessed to have been able to go back to work at the Pizza Hut, I wanted to do something more. I was soon blessed with a terrific job working with mentally challenged adults. I worked on weekends only, from Saturday morning at 7:00 am until Monday morning at 9:00 am so I could be with the children all week as well. I taught the residents simple tasks like tying their shoe laces to preparing simple meals for themselves. I took them out to movies or shopping in hopes of teaching them social skills. I loved this work because it made me feel like I was really making a difference. I could even bring Boobie and Cherylyn to work with me for short visits. I no longer needed food stamps and I loved the feeling of being able to provide for my family. It was really great. I was making good money and I decided that my children deserved to be in a real home, not some make shift place. I told Tyrone that with our income tax refund, we would buy a trailer. He wasn't too enthused over the idea but I had made up my mind that my children deserved to be raised in a more comfortable environment just as I had been. I decided that I would pursue my dream of being a nurse too. I enrolled in a community college in the fall and started taking the prerequisites for the nursing program. I loved school and I loved interacting with other people. I loved learning and I was very proud of my choice. I finished all of my prerequisites and was accepted into the nursing program that fall. I was so happy that finally, I would not just have a job, but a career, one that I could take anywhere in the country and find work without much worry. Tyrone must have known this too. He began to try to make my life more of a living hell. It seemed that every time I would come home midday to prepare a care plan or my drug cards for clinical that evening, he would come and start a fight over nothing, anything.

Despite the personal torment I went through, almost consistently, I stayed focused on a trailer for my children. When we filed taxes that year, I bought a very nice, single wide trailer. All the instincts inside of me were screaming, "Leave Tyrone behind." Would you believe that after everything, I still loved him? He moved with us in our new trailer. I had never been prouder than the moment we moved. There were only two bedrooms but finally, our children had a real home. It really was a terrific trailer too!

I continued to go to school but I guess Tyrone must have felt threatened. He did everything in his power to discourage me from continuing my education. I ignored him and studied that much harder. I continued to work at the Group Home on weekends as well and it was neither hard nor physical work so I was blessed anyway. Then, in my second semester, I found out I was pregnant again. It had been five and a half years since I had a baby and I found myself very happy despite my rocky marriage. I had come to expect that my marriage would just be like this until my Tyrone became sanctified. Tyrone seemed happy that we were having another baby as well and I was quite surprised with his reaction, being that he really "only wanted one." Looking at it now, I guess he thought that being pregnant again would surely sabotage any dreams of completing nursing school. Psych!!

Chapter 11

A s it turned out, about my 3rd month carrying my baby, I developed something called placenta previa. That was, as I understood it then, a situation where the placenta was out of its normal place in my uterus. It was in front of the inside of my uterus and if I didn't take it easy and stay off my feet as much as possible, I could loose the baby or my life for that matter. So needless to say, I walked to my nursing professor's office very down trodden. I felt very disappointed with myself. I remember thinking that I wouldn't miss dissecting those smelly cats in Anatomy and Physiology though. Anyway, I sat there looking down at the floor as I told her what the doctor had told me. "Ms. Bigg, I can't come back to school right now. I have placenta previa and I have to drop out." As I begin to cry Ms. Bigg said, "Cheryl, you're not happy in your marriage are you?" I stopped crying as I stared at her with amazement. I never answered her question. Then she broke the silence by saying to me, "You're a very smart person. You just have to remember that the world does not revolve around you. When you decide to come back, you'll do just fine." I remember leaving her office that day wondering, "Is my unhappiness that obvious and have I displayed an attitude of being that needy of a person?" So, I was forced to drop out of school while pregnant with my third child. I got a lot of rest, took my prenatal vitamins religiously and thanks to a good job, ate very well-balanced meals. Someone had told me about a WIC program where I could get cereal, milk, juices, cheese and I must say that was a blessing not only for me, but for my babies as well. I enjoyed being home with Tyrone Jr. and Cherylyn. It was good to be at home when they came home from school too. I loved to have their dinner ready and hear about their daily adventures. Tyrone had even started doing much better with the bills. He continued to stay away from home more than he stayed at home. I missed the fantasy of having a happy home, but soon I found more comfort in him not being at home. It had gotten to be that when I heard the car's motor pull into the trailer court, it felt like a big cinder block was pressing down on my chest.

My pregnancy progressed without further complications and in March, I was blessed with Michael. Michael was a bundle of joy. He was always the happiest, great spirited little boy. He was a good baby. He rarely cried. As he grew, he became a very busy little fellow. He didn't require very much prompting to do the things one would teach most babies to do, i.e., sit alone, crawl, etc. One day, Boobie, Cherylyn and I were all sitting in the living room watching tv. Out of no where came Michael, crawling up the hallway with the widest grin on his face. I was very surprised to see him because at four months, no one had taught him to crawl yet. Then, I thought, I had put him in the crib for a nap. How did he manage to get out of the crib? Well, I went into the bedroom to investigate. What I found was that Michael had torn a few rails from the siding of the crib and made a space just big enough for him to get through. I was amazed at this little busy, happy guy. As I went back into the living room, there was Michael crawling around on the floor, still with this big ole smile on his little face, playing with his siblings. I patched the railing back up as best as I could. My patchwork held for a couple months. One evening, we were sitting in the kitchen eating dinner, when, up the hallway walks little six month old Michael. He was laughing as he made his way to me at the table. Michael was quite pleased with his new found skill of walking. As I investigated Michael's escape route, he had again, torn the rails out of the crib. The more I patched the crib rails, the more Michael found ways to rip them out again. I finally gave up. Michael was, indeed, hyperactive, starting at 4 months of his life.

As the months went on, Michael grew and became busier and busier. Tyrone was hardly ever home and when he was, he rarely spent quality time or any other time with the children. Michael's curiosity level about everything grew. He never slowed down. He had long since stopped taking naps during the day. He would not even sit long enough for meals. We would just wait for Michael to run to and from the dinner table to put food in his mouth. He was truly a handful but we all loved him dearly. It had been almost six years since a baby had been in the house. In later years, I began to affectionately refer to Michael as "my character builder."

Chapter 12

I noticed one Monday morning as I came home from work that the family portrait that hung just above the sofa in the living room was not there. I went over to the sofa and looked around and behind it. Sure enough, there was the picture. I hung it back on the wall. Then I began to notice that every Monday morning, the family's picture would not be on the wall. When I asked Tyrone about it he said, "Cherylyn put that behind there." I thought it very strange that she would be putting the picture behind the sofa in the first place and then only on the weekends but I asked her anyway. She said, "Momma, I didn't do it." After about the fourth time of hanging the picture up again, I really fussed at Cherylyn and I threatened to beat her behind. She started crying hysterically as she said over and over again "But momma, I didn't do it, I didn't do it!" Tyrone kept insisting that she did do it. Finally, I just took the picture down altogether.

It was Christmas time. Tyrone always took all of us on boring shopping trips that I dreaded. We would never shop in town; instead, we would go miles and miles from home to do our shopping. He never wanted to take the children inside the stores either. Instead he made them stay inside the car. I hated that he did that. All I could think of was why doesn't he let the children go, doesn't he know how bored they must be? I never said anything to him though. I just went miserably along with him. Tyrone announced that this Christmas, he could not buy us gifts because he was exchanging gifts with his co-workers at the hospital and he would buy us gifts after Christmas. I thought it was very unusual that he should have to buy so many gifts to exchange with co-workers but I went along with it anyway. I helped him pick out lap robes, cooking utensils, blankets, and lots of really nice gifts. True to his word, Christmas came and went and we, his immediate family did not receive any gifts. Needless to say, the children were very unhappy that Tyrone had nothing to give them from him on Christmas morning. I would always try to compensate for his shortcomings, even if it meant neglecting things that I may have really needed, and this time was no different. I made sure the little ones had something if it wasn't exactly what they wanted. After all, Tyrone had spent his entire paycheck on his fellow co-workers.

I was sitting home on one clear, winter day in February. These two ladies drove up and one of them got out of the car and knocked on the door. When I answered it she said, "Are you the lady of this house?" I said, "Yes I am. Who wants to know?" She then asked if she could come in. I, of course allowed her to. After I asked her to please sit down, she started talking, boy did she ever start talking. She said, "I come over to your house every weekend." She said that she came to my house, this house, every weekend and Tyrone told her he just stayed here for the weekend to keep his cousin's kids, our kids. She then described the entire trailer to me and her description was exact. She said that Tyrone had given her an engagement ring for Christmas and he was supposed to marry her after Christmas. I actually begin to feel sorry for Yvette. She went on to say that Tyrone had given her grandparents and her really nice gifts for Christmas. All of the things that she described were the things that I had walked around the stores helping him pick out "for the coworkers." She even described my parent's home to me, inside and out. She said that Tyrone had taken her there as well. I now knew what really happened with the family picture every weekend. She decided to wait until Tyrone came home from work so she could confront him in my presence. When we heard him drive up, Yvette decided to hide in the closet. Tyrone came through the doorway whistling, just as happy as he could be. I asked him, "Tyrone, who is Yvette Cooker?" to which he replied with the largest wrinkle in his forehead that you could imagine, "Yvette Cooker, Yvette Cooker, I don't know any Yvette Cooker." Well, at that moment, Yvette bursts out of the closet, all 6'2, and 230 something pounds of her. She was pushing up against 5'5 and 140 something pounds of Tyrone. She starting hitting him while asking him, "Oh, you don't know who I am huh, you forgot me huh?" She kicked his butt royally that day, all up and down that trailer. The whole thing was quite hilarious to me. Anyway, after this latest escapade with Yvette Cooker, why I continued to stay with Tyrone, only God knows, because I don't. Tyrone's butt beating that he had just voluntarily accepted from Yvette brought back to mind a saying mom used often. She always referred to people who went around messing with only those individuals they thought they could overcome without any problems as being "An indoor bully and an outdoor coward." From that day on, I viewed Tyrone just as mom's saying depicted.

I was sitting in the office of the Group Home one Saturday evening. I was reading a book and Boobie and Cherylyn were playing quietly on the floor. All of a sudden, there was a loud scream followed by banging on the office door. When I opened it, there was one of the female residents standing there as a male resident was grabbing for her. There was blood on the office door as well. I pulled the female inside of the office and slammed the door. The male resident continued to beat on the door. I was so frantic and scared; scared for the female, my little ones and myself. I picked up the telephone and called the police. Thank God they responded so quickly. It seemed that within 5 minutes, the police were there. They took the male resident away in handcuffs. It seems that the male had given the female a dollar. She had gone across the street to the little neighborhood store and bought a honey bun for herself and a soda for one of the other male residents. This really ticked the guy off and he stabbed her in her hand with some scissors. It obviously was a really big deal to this guy. This incident really shook me up. After it was all over, I kept thinking of all the horrible things that could have happened that day. I resigned my job shortly after that. I decided that I would go back to nursing school. I wondered if Tyrone was upset about my resignation. After all, my not working anymore on the weekends messed his weekend escapades up too didn't it?

Chapter 13

Well, here I was, pregnant with Tyrone's 4th child. Although it was another very stressful and unhappy pregnancy and period in my life, I gave birth to a healthy baby boy 23 months after Michael's birth. I named him John Lee, after my dear father. He was the largest of my children, weighing in at 9lbs, 6.5oz. He was a good-natured baby. He was a good baby too. I was quite surprised with his temperament, considering how Tyrone had seen to it that I stay continuously upset and stressed throughout the pregnancy. He rarely came home and after my giving birth to John Lee, he was no different. I was hoping he would help me to take care of the others while I recuperated from having John Lee. I tried to breastfeed the three before John Lee, quite unsuccessfully I might add. I had no better luck with John Lee. When I came home from the hospital, my breasts were so swollen, sore and very hard. They felt as hard as little stones, no; make that BIG stones, in my chest. I could not put my arms down by my sides when I walked. I'm sure I looked like Herman Munster, yet again, when I tried to walk. The doctor had written a prescription for some Parlodel, a drug used back in the day to dry the breast milk and inhibit further production of it. Those pills had worked miracles before with my breast engorgements and I needed them desperately now. I asked Tyrone early in the morning if he would go to the drug store to pick them up for me. I didn't see him again until very late that night. I wasn't feeling very much like doing anything but what does one do when you have four little ones depending on you? I knew the children were hungry so I pulled a chair up to the stove. I remember feeling weak and dizzy but, by God's grace and mercy, I managed to prepare breakfast for my kids. I always enjoyed watching them eat because I remembered not so long ago; we didn't have the food readily available to eat. Anyway, I went back to bed after making sure all of my little ones were well fed. Dad came over to see me at lunch time and I know God sent him. He came with a picnic basket with lots of good food he had prepared. He was a really great cook and we all enjoyed the food very much. Dad also told me about steaming some cabbage or collard leaves and placing them on my breasts to relieve the throbbing pain and swelling. I never knew that and I was quite amazed that Dad knew about things like that. My wonderful next door neighbors, Mrs. Ruby and her husband, always planted a garden and had lots of collards. Mrs. Ruby also ran a little store and that little store proved to be a God send to me and my little ones. I would send Boobie over to her store with a note when we were low on or out of groceries and she would always come through for us. I sent him over with a note on this day and she again, came through. Dad steamed the collard leaves and I placed them on my breasts. It wasn't instant relief but as the evening passed on, I felt much better. When Tyrone finally came home, I said, "Tyrone, I have been so sick. I needed my medicine and I needed you to take care of

the children." He replied, "I don't know why you're so sick, all
you did was have a baby." I was so hurt by his obvious lack of
caring. I didn't reply to his statement but I remember wishing
he could be made to push a 9lb., 6-1/2 oz. something, anything,
out of his body so he could see if he wouldn't feel sick too. Later, when I thought about the children that Tyrone and I had together, I realized that Tyrone only went into the delivery room
with me once, which was with Boobie. I can't remember him
being there with me with Cherylyn but perhaps he was. With
the two other babies, I labored and delivered them without his
presence for sure. Now, thinking back on things, I also drove
myself home from the hospital after delivering the last three
children as well. I thank God for mom though because she was
always right there by my side. I know she didn't feel well at all
when I delivered John Lee though. I labored alone and I kept
calling dad and asking for mom. He would always tell me she
was on her way. Shortly after I delivered, I heard her footsteps
slowly sliding down the hallway. That sound was the sweetest sound I'd ever heard in my life at that moment. A mother's
love is surely the next best thing to God's.

Not all of the time was Tyrone unpleasant to be around.
He'd like to take the children and me to places like national
parks and have cook-outs. He also liked to fish so we'd go fishing. I'd had enough of fishing hanging around with mom so
I didn't like that but I went along anyway, for the children.
Then, I remember on one occasion he took us to King's Domin-
ion. It's a huge amusement park that is lots and lots of fun. I
had our four children and Doll's two children with us. Tyrone
paid our way in the park, told me to hold the car keys as he
got the money for the tickets out of his pocket. There was this
very attractive lady in the line next to us. She had a very nice
body and she had on this fishnet shorts outfit that was very

revealing. Tyrone, of course, noticed her too. After paying for the tickets, as we went inside the park, he suddenly forgot something. He told me to "stand right here, I'll be right back." The kids and I stood there for about 20 minutes or so before I realized this was just another one of his lame pranks. At least he was thoughtful enough to have, very cunningly, left me the car keys. Tyrone left me there with all the children, no money for snacks, games, those shaved ice drinks that the kids love, nothing. Thank God I cooked and packed a large meal complete with snacks and drinks and placed in the trunk of the car just before leaving. Anyway, we walked around and the children rode fun rides, took in all the sights and had a good time. I just walked around thinking how low down he was to do me and the kids like this. About an hour or so before the park closed, Tyrone came running up to me. "Where in the world have y'all been? I've been looking for y'all everywhere," he said as he approached us. I didn't even dignify that with an answer. The good that he did was totally outweighed by the bad, that's for sure.

Chapter 14

Even though Tyrone and I were on again, off again, mostly off again, he did provide a car for me to drive. I guess he must have figured that I couldn't very well walk around town with four children and shopping bags. Whatever his reason, I was very thankful for transportation. The cars were not always so reliable but Tyrone had started to tinker with auto mechanics, so he kept me puttering along. I was still focused on completing nursing school but having the four little ones to care for proved more difficult than I expected. I knew that mom would help me with the children. Having Boobie and Cherylyn in school was helpful too. So, I applied to the nursing school that was local, right in my hometown. This was not a program for registered nurses; instead it was for practical nurses. Even though Tyrone provided a car for me to drive, I did not want to trust that, if I attempted going out of town to school again, he would not take the car or attempt some other stunt. I figured if I went to school locally, I could take a taxi or walk if necessary, to my classes. I received my letter in the spring of the year. I had indeed been accepted to nursing school to start in the fall of the year. All I remember saying was "Thank you God, oh how I thank you God" over and over again. I wasn't sure where the money for tuition, books, uniforms, and anything else was coming from but I only needed the faith the size of a mustard seed and I sure had that. I told mom and dad and they were excited for me as well. Mom agreed to watch Michael and John Lee for me and dad surprisingly agreed that Boobie and Cherylyn could ride the bus to their house after school on the days that I had clinical. Everything was working out just fine, except, the funding. There was no need to ask Tyrone for the money because I knew I stood a better chance of getting blood from a turnip.

I was bound and determined that I was going to school in the fall. I have a very dear first cousin that I visited often, and still, to this day, continue to visit. Her name is Mae. Although she is somewhat older than I am, we were still good friends. One particular day in the summer, I went over to see her. She knew a lot of people and was very resourceful. I asked if she knew anyone who would loan me about $500.00. She thought and thought for a while. Finally she said, "Cheryl, you know I would give it to you if I had it. I know this man who would loan it to you. I'll give you his number." I was beside myself with joy at this news. I thanked her and immediately went home to call this man. His name was Burt. Thankfully he answered the telephone on the second ring. I introduced myself and surprisingly, he said, "I know who you are. I know your whole family." He then said that we should meet and discuss this loan. Excitedly, I asked him if I could come to his place of business to meet with him, thinking all the time he was a loan officer or someone equivalent. To my surprise, he says "I'll meet you in the park 5:00 pm tomorrow evening." Well, little naive me; I didn't think anything about this set up but "I'm going to school in the fall."

True to his word, Burt met me in the park promptly at 5:00. Although I had lived in this town all of my life, I cannot remember ever seeing this man before. Where I was usually quite shy and reserved, going to school meant so much to me that I had no problem getting to the point. I told him I needed to borrow 500 dollars to go to nursing school and I would pay him back in small increments until I finished school, with interest of course. He had very piercing eyes and they were focused directly on me as I spoke. When I was finished talking, he said, "I'll give you 250 dollars now and 250 before school starts. You don't have to pay me back but I do want to see you again." I was at a loss for words. I had not expected this from Burt and I had never thought about cheating on Tyrone either, yet, I found myself quite intrigued by this dark stranger with the dark, piercing eyes. I know that I was very vulnerable too. I had become accustomed to getting very little, positive attention from a man for the past 10 years. Anyway, he gave me two one hundred dollar bills and a fifty and told me to give him my telephone number. I did. I thanked him for the money and he walked me back to my car from the park. Being so naïve, I knew that he wanted to see me again because he told me so. I, however, wasn't sure what else was involved. I thanked him and drove off. I didn't see him again for about two weeks.

I paid for the tuition with the $250.00 that Burt had given me. I was beside myself with excitement. I needed to be fitted for my uniforms and I needed money for the uniforms at the fitting. I also needed money for my books and white shoes for clinical. I hadn't heard from Burt but I didn't want to call him. After all, he said he would call me. I didn't want to seem desperate, although I was. On the day before my fitting was scheduled, Burt called. Despite myself, I found myself being very glad to hear from him again. He said he wanted to see me. Tyrone was at work, so I asked mom if she would watch the children for me for a couple of hours. She did. I drove to this secluded looking area where Burt suggested I meet him. When I parked the car, I didn't see him. Then suddenly, out of nowhere, he appeared. There was something very mystical about this man but I was no less intrigued by him. He walked up to the car and opened the door and beckoned for me to get out. When I did, he gave me the tightest hug and warmest kiss I had gotten in a very long time. My, how good his arms felt, how good his lips tasted. As we talked, I learned that he was married and immediately, I felt condemned. My conscious was immediately killing me. All I could think of was, "I'm no better than the women Tyrone is messing around with on me." He must have seen the look of condemnation on my face, in my eyes because he immediately began to console me. He talked really soft and stroked my hair and the center of my back as he went on to tell me that he loved his wife and I wasn't coming between them. He said he just wanted to help me out and give me some love that I had been missing. I don't know how he knew but he sure hit the nail on the head. I told him that I needed the rest of the money by tomorrow because I had to purchase my uniform and books. He immediately pulled four one hundred dollar bills out of his wallet and folded them in my hands. Then he said "Buy your children something with the rest of the money." I think I must have fallen in love with him right then and there. Thus, a whirlwind affair started.

Chapter 15

It was finally September and nursing school started. True to mom and dad's promise, they kept Michael and John Lee for me. The first year of school only lasted until 11:30 am so I was able to pick them up early and go home to prepare dinner for us. I enjoyed school and I had a great bunch of school mates. Learning was fun and interesting and my instructors were really sweet too. There were three of them and ironically, they were biological sisters, yet they were all very different. One was the diplomatic type, very serious and strong-willed. One was very gentle and soft-spoken, with a very compassionate mannerism about her. The other one was very loud, very funny and she made classroom very fun as we learned. The three of them made for a very well-rounded learning experience. Home life was much more relaxed and enjoyable and I attribute a large portion of that to Burt. We saw each other a lot and I took the children with us on most of our rendezvous. He always gave me plenty of money and plenty of much needed, good loving. I was totally taken with this man but my thoughts always came back to the fact that he was married and my conscious would end up whipping me to no end. It's funny though. As soon as he would call to ask me to meet him somewhere, I would find a way to be there. Tyrone had started acting better now. He would put the children on the bus in the morning and keep John Lee at home with him. Some days when I came home from school, he would have put John Lee to sleep and be lying out in the bed stark naked, waiting for me. When I came inside and saw him like that, I had no desire whatsoever to be with him. My needs were all totally taken care of thanks to Burt and I know that Tyrone sensed this. I didn't have sex with him very often because I simply wasn't interested anymore. On the rare occasions that I did have sex with him, I cannot say make love because I feel that no love was ever made where we are concerned, I would think of Burt. Sometimes in the middle of these sessions, he would say, "Cheryl, what in the world are you thinking about." I would simply reply, "Nothing." On those occasions where Tyrone became angry with me for unbelievably not having any interest in him, he would start arguments and fights. I've had to send Boobie to Ms. Ruby's to call 911 on several occasions. I was tired of Tyrone fighting me so I remember getting one of Orlando's old guns once. It was as rusty as it could be but I loaded it anyway. I had no idea of how to shoot it but I was desperate. Sure enough, Tyrone started in on me in the hallway of our little trailer. I went to get the gun and when I came back, I pointed it at him. I said, "Start something." He stopped arguing immediately and says in a normal tone of voice, "Go on now Cheryl, stop playing." I knew right then he knew I wasn't playing. I'm glad I didn't pull the trigger because as rusty and old as that gun was, it probably would have backfired and I would have shot myself. Besides, I didn't want his blood or anyone else's on my hands. Tyrone might not have been exactly sure as to what was going on but my mom, with her intuitive self, certainly was. I remember her saying to me once, "Cheryl, who in the world is this man you're seeing?" I just gave her one of those stupid looks.

Chapter 16

School was progressing very well. I sailed through my first year with straight A's. I could finally see the light at the end of the tunnel for my little ones and me. I only had another year to go. Mom wasn't feeling well lately. I noticed that she would sit in a chair in the dining room and look out of the window for the most part of the day. She'd always enjoyed cooking and she was an excellent cook. She had always enjoyed gardening, sewing and looking back now, I don't see how she managed to take care of six children, a very demanding husband, cook three hot, delicious meals everyday, sew for all of us and keep an immaculate house and the most beautiful yard in the neighborhood, but she did. Ethel Mae was truly and extraordinary woman. Anyway, she loved to go fishing and almost every time she did and didn't manage to make it home before dad arrived, he would fuss nonstop. Dad fussed all the time, nonstop. I remember as a little girl, mom worked as a nurse on the "graveyard" shift. Dad would fuss and fuss and fuss about that until finally, mom just started to stay home at nights. I remember mom saying to dad on several occasions,

"Honey, I get so tired of you fussing and nagging at me." On those occasions where she must have been really pissed off at him, I remember her putting her spoon in her coffee cup and slinging some hot coffee over on him. Dad would just sit there quietly then. Anyway, mom worked very hard in her lifetime. Although I didn't really realize what depression really was then, I now believe that mom was very depressed. Where she always took great care of her personal self, she would now allow her appearance to go lacking, as well as her personal hygiene. Where her food was always finger licking- good, she would now burn her foods more often than not. Well, dad obviously didn't understand depression either, because he came home from work and immediately started fussing with mom.

Surprisingly, mom started coming out of her depression just as abruptly as it seemed to overtake her initially. Where she had not been very active in church services and speaking on church topics, she now started again. I would enjoy sitting there listening to her teach on any given topic. Just sitting there looking at the smile on her face as she would go on with her teachings made me realize just how much she loved the Lord and what she was doing. We started being hanging buddies again. I would take her out of the house and we would stay for most of the day. We'd go shopping, out to eat, just riding and sight-seeing. This was good for me and mom. She was my very best friend. It was really great to see mom getting back into the swing of life.

It was the Saturday before Easter. I was putting a perm in mom's hair. She was quiet by nature but she was unusually quiet this day. I asked her how she felt. She said she was fine. I have never in my entire life heard mom complain about anything! This time was no different. After I rolled her hair, she went to lie down. I went home to prepare the children's clothes and Cherylyn's hair for church. When I arrived at moms on Easter Sunday morning, I discovered she had fallen getting into the car to go to church. She was in the hospital in the intensive care unit. She actually had a stroke on Saturday and some of the effect of it showed on the next day. When I went in her room, she was lying there in bed trying to talk to me. Her speech was very slurred but I could still understand her for the most part. There she was, hardly able to speak clearly, yet, telling me how pretty I looked. She still did not complain. I felt so very bad for her. She stayed in the hospital for a while. Then dad agreed with her doctor to send her about 200 miles west to a rehabilitation center. Dad, the children and I would drive through the mountains every week to see her. I didn't much like driving in the mountains but the scenery was breathtakingly beautiful. Most importantly, I had to check on mom. Mom had been very inactive even before the stroke so I didn't feel that rehabilitation was a realistic goal for her. I remember hating so much to leave mom at the end of our visits. I knew she couldn't feed herself, go to the bathroom for herself and she couldn't speak well or hear well. It would really break my heart into to leave her. I could see that it broke dad's heart too. After about a month, dad decided that he would bring her home and in his words, "Take care of her and do the best I can for her if I fall off my feet trying." That is what he did. He did a great job with mom. I helped out as much as I could. I went to school and afterwards the children and I would come to their house to help dad with mom.

That fall, Evelyn and her husband Mike came home with their four little ones, the youngest being two years old. They had just come back from Germany. She was very concerned about mom and wanted to come to stay with mom and dad for a while and help them out. After a couple weeks, Mike went on to Colorado to resume his military duties and to set up a home for them there. I was very glad to have her home with all of us. She enrolled her children in school and set to work cleaning the house, doing the grocery shopping and general house shopping, cooking three hot meals everyday, just as dad loved. When Mike sent her money, she would put the majority of it right into dad's household. One would think that Dad would have been happy but he wasn't. He continued to fuss, complain, and find fault in anything, everything. It seemed that mom or his children could never do anything to please this man. I guess if we had pulled our heads off and handed it over to him, he would have fussed that we didn't do that just right either. I remember coming home from school one day only to find Evelyn very sick. She was planning to re-paint the kitchen, dining and living rooms to brighten up the house some. She had been up on a ladder scraping old paint from the ceiling in the kitchen when she became very faint. She went to the bathroom and sat down on the toilet to try to regain her composure. She still felt bad so she called dad to come and help her to get up. She said "Dad came and said he couldn't help me to get up but he would call the ambulance service for me." Well, the ambulance came and carried her to the hospital. There she found out that her blood pressure was very high and they held her there until her blood pressure lowered some. After she came back home, she said she was hoping dad had finished cooking for mom, her and her family and himself. Dad was an excellent cook for sure. Instead, what she found was that dad had placed a chair in front of the stove for her to sit down in as she prepared the meal. How very thoughtful huh? Well, when I arrived at dad's that evening, I was royally PISSED! He was retired from carpentry now and just did odd jobs for people around town. He mostly stayed home though and when he wasn't in his study or listening to his radio; he was working in his vegetable garden in between fussing. The housework and taking care of dad and mom was a huge job and it was way too much for Evelyn. John Lee, Jr. began to send money to hire a housekeeper and he continued to send money for years. I later learned that John Lee, Jr. put himself in quite a financial strain trying to help dad and mom. Doll paid mom and dad's supplemental insurance for years and years and she continued until there was no further need to. For the most part, my sisters and brothers came together to help my aging parents. I cannot say what Orlando and David's contributions were because I cannot recall them doing very much of anything. Martha, Tyrone's mom, begin to work for mom and dad thanks to John Lee, Jr. She came over, almost everyday, and cooked and cleaned for them and we were all pleased with Martha, even Dad. Evelyn was pleased to have the company and the help too. I know it must have been lonely around the house for Evelyn. Mom was not able to be very talkative and Dad was in his study most of the day. Her children were in school, as was I, so Martha was a welcomed sight I'm sure.

I was glad to have my big sister home with me as well. I would come over some evenings after school and sit and talk with her for hours and hours. I was so happy, for the most part, in this new found affair that I had going on and I confided in Evelyn about it. I had already told my sister Doll about him and once, when she had come home to visit, she had met him. We all went out skating that night and had a wonderful time. Doll liked him immediately. Anyway, Evelyn didn't say anything. I suppose I didn't give her the chance to say much because I was talking so much about him. I told her that the only drawback to this whole thing was he was married and I felt very badly about that. I went on to tell her where he worked, some of the places he would take me and the kids, just a lot of stuff about him. I was so excited to feel loved and I wanted her to share in my excitement. She listened to me very intently. I think it was about a week later. Tyrone came to me and said, "I know who you're seeing Cheryl." Of course, I was dumbfounded. He went on to tell me everything. I never admitted to any of it. I used to tell Tyrone, "You're giving me up for adoption." His only reply would be, "Go on and do what you want. I don't care." So, I really didn't feel I owed him an explanation or anything else for that matter. As it turned out, all of the things that I had shared with Evelyn, somehow Martha, my own mother-n-law found out as well. I suppose being so lonesome during the days at mom's house, Evelyn just lost herself in Martha's deceptive company and emptied her guts to her. I still could not understand that though. Needless to say, this whirlwind romance was over, not right away, but soon thereafter. During the short time that we did continue to see each other, things were never quite the same. Finally, we mutually decided that enough was enough. When I asked Evelyn why she told my mother- in-law of all people, she said, "Cheryl, Martha told me, I didn't tell her." Of course I didn't believe her. It did turn out to be a blessing in disguise though. My conscious sure felt better.

Chapter 17

It was early spring. Evelyn and her children were preparing to leave to meet Mike. I was sorry to see her go. Even though she had ratted me out, my love for her went unchanged. We were always close and still are. Nursing school continued to progress well and my children were growing like little weeds. They seemed to be growing so fast. Tyrone and I were still living in the same house but I made it clear that as soon as I was finished with school, if he didn't leave, I would, with the children. Who would believe that loving someone the way that I'd loved Tyrone could ever change, could ever die? I did learn one very important lesson. It takes two people to be in love. Love doesn't work too well when you're in it by yourself. The trailer, once beautiful, had become a mere shell of a house. Tyrone was very good at tearing things up, but he saw no need in repairing them. He would work on motors in the kitchen floor, drilling holes right through the floor as he worked. He would never patch them up though. There was a leak in the kitchen sink, which in turn escalated into some of the kitchen flooring rotting out. Since he had only placed

makeshift tin around the outside of the house, there was not
much protection from the weather and one could stand right
in the kitchen and look down at the ground. Yes, the little trailer was in need of much repairing. The furnace was not working properly either. When we turned the thermostat up for the
furnace to come on, it would smoke up the entire house. Tyrone did get two kerosene heaters for us. We placed one in the
living room and one in the back bedroom where the children
and I slept.

After Evelyn left I still continued to help dad out with mom.
I would cook dinner for them. I or Cherylyn would bathe her
every night and because mom could not have a normal bowel
movement, Cherylyn or I would put her on her bedside commode and manually stimulate her so that she could have one.
Tyrone even helped out with mom sometimes. Before mom
had gotten sick, she actually started to like Tyrone. When I
came to her with one thing or another about us, she would just
sit there and listen quietly. Then she would say, "Work it out
if you can." I guess she had gotten used to me and Tyrone's
ongoing drama. I managed school and dad's household; how
I couldn't say. I hardly ever was at my house because I was at
moms, me and the kids. I continued my quest to do well in
school even with my new and very hectic schedule. I hardly
ever saw Tyrone but that was okay.

I suppose Tyrone suspected that, for once in my life, I was
really serious about ending this play marriage we'd kept going for almost twelve years. Before, we always ended up fighting, only to end up back together. Anyway, he came home one
day and told me, "Cheryl, I'm going to move away. I want to
be happy just like you do." I thought to myself, "If he hasn't
been happy for the past eleven years, he's certainly put on one
hell of a façade." I was in total agreement with this though.

Sure enough, he took a few belongings and left town. He left his job at the local hospital and my sister-n-law Queeta said he moved to the Tidewater area. At any rate, I could not miss what I never had so life went on.

Tyrone continued to send money but it became very sporadic, then it stopped altogether. I had to actually file a child support petition to have him come to court to set up child support payments. He did show up for court from the Tidewater area or so he said. That day, child support was set up, along with him being ordered to pay half of the children's medical and dental bills. He did mail the ordered amount for a while. He'd never had any kind of health insurance on his family so he never paid half or any other percentage for those expenses. Things were more difficult but I had to hang in there, for me and my children.

Chapter 18

Mom always had such a great sense of humor. She could have you cracking your sides laughing at her as she would go on and on without as much as a smile. She was especially funny when she was fussing with one of us. It was very hard not to laugh most of the time. My children say the same things about me now. I know exactly where that sense of humor came from. Mom had the funniest sayings too. She always said, "Cheryl, remember, every shut eye ain't sleep and every goodbye ain't gone." She would also compare something that happened very fast as lasting as long as "Pat stayed in the army." I don't know who Pat was or how long they stayed in the army but I gathered it wasn't very long. That's about how long Tyrone stayed gone. He came back later in the year, around late fall. He lived with Martha and he was able to get his old job back at the hospital. He was really good at what he did. The best part is that I was able to pick the child support up directly from the hospital every payday. I continued going to school and my little ones continued to grow and grow. I hated that they didn't have a father in their lives and I tried to encourage Tyrone to be a part of their lives. They loved their father and were eager to spend time with him. I would call Martha's and tell Tyrone that I was bringing the children over to spend some time with him. I would drop them off and it wouldn't be so long before he was calling to tell me to come pick them up.

The trailer was steadily falling apart and I was putting all the money I had into feeding and clothing the children, buying oil for the kerosene heaters, buying school supplies for me and the kids, whatever. I was going to school full- time, I was being both mom and dad; I was helping out with my mom and dad; I was overwhelmed! Out of all of what was going on, I had a peace of mind. I didn't have to argue, fight, loose sleep as I tossed and turned in bed some nights wondering where my husband was and if he were coming home; none of that and I thank God for it. Times were hard, but through it all, God kept us even when I didn't realize it.

Boobie and Cherylyn were such good, helpful children. On those late evenings when I had clinicals, they would be at home with Michael and John Lee alone. I would always make sure they had a good meal already cooked before I left for the hospital. Those two little ones would take good care of each other and their two younger siblings. I didn't like the idea of leaving them alone with the kerosene heaters. The trailer was very much unsecure and very drafty too. I would tell God, "God, You know I'm doing the very best that I can. Please look down on my children and keep them in Your care." I would then go on to handle my business at the hospital. I knew that I had to get through this period so that I could make a better, more comfortable life for my children and me.

Chapter 19

It was early December and I was in the last leg of nursing school. We were coming up on exams leading to Christmas break. I was doing very well. I'd made all A's so far. We were now going to clinicals during the day and some evenings. We had a patient and we assumed their care from start to finish. We were on the medical/surgical floor and there was this little cute, young nurse that was the charge nurse there. I had a very close friend in school named Laura. She had rheumatoid arthritis that was a result of being in a very serious car accident but she was a real fighter. Anyway, she told me one day that Tyrone was having an affair with Angel, the charge nurse. I was shocked. I was angry. I was embarrassed. Tyrone had been saying lately that he missed us. I had not succumbed to his wooing but I was hoping that he did want to build and maintain closeness with our children.

A few weeks before Christmas, Tyrone came to the house. He had not gotten all of his things out of the house and he said he came to tell me he was going to get them. He also said, "Cheryl, I met this lady. She's a nurse. Her name is Angel and we're going to have a child together. I love her very much and we're going to get married. She works at the hospital and I just wanted you to know." Well, what a fine time to tell me. It seemed I was the last one to know. This entire time, my classmates knew all about Angel but for whatever their reasons, never told me until Laura told me. I was very angry that for weeks, this nurse was there on her floor, watching me, thinking who knows what, as I'm there going on my merry way blindly. I think I was more embarrassed than anything else. Just before exams, I went into a deep state of depression. I knew that Tyrone was never supportive of me going back to school or much of anything else I did so I felt like this was his last ditch effort to hold me down, to discourage me. It was working too. Then, on the fourth day of missing class just before exams, Doll called me. She said "Girl, why are you at home? Why aren't you in school?" I replied, "I just haven't felt like it." She replied, "Girl, if you don't get up and get your behind in school tomorrow, I'm going to come down there and kick it all over the place." This got my attention let me tell you. Out of all the years I had known Doll, she had only been seriously stern with me once. Then Laura came over. She said, "Girl, if you don't come back to school you had better. You can't let Tyrone and nobody else stop you from reaching your goals. You know you're almost finished, don't throw it away now." Well, I thank God for them because they really pulled me out of that depressive state in a hurry, a big hurry. I went back to school that very next day. My classmates were very careful to try to look and act normal and I appreciate them for it even to this day. I managed to do well on my exams and keep a sense of balance for the kid's sake that only God could have provided. True enough, Angel did have a baby, a little girl I heard. I've never seen this little girl, nor have my children. Tyrone didn't marry her though despite his proclamation of unyielding love for her.

Finally, the big day arrived. It was April and I had, by God's grace and mercy, completed nursing school and with an A average too. I invited Tyrone to the graduation ceremony. I think I did this more for any other reason, so that he could see that I did finish school, despite his lack of support. Dad was there and so was mom, in her wheelchair. My brothers John Lee, Orlando and David, Evelyn, and of course, the children were there too. Doll could not make the trip from Texas but she sent her well wishes. My entire family was very proud of me and I was proud of myself. I had finally finished something I started. Half way through the ceremony Tyrone strutted in. I guess he wanted to make sure everyone saw him, I really don't know. Anyway, after everything was over, each of the graduate nurses were given roses as we walked off the stage. As I was leaving the auditorium, I leaned over and kissed mom on her cheek and gave her my roses. She had not come to my high school graduation nor my wedding and finally, I had accomplished something she was proud to come to and be a part of. Mom deserved a lot more than just simple roses for putting up with all of my mistakes since adolescence and loving me just the same! Tyrone came over to congratulate me as well. He later came over to the trailer and we had sex as a "graduation gift." I still had some feelings for Tyrone, though I'm not sure what they were. I guess some sort of feelings were still there mainly because he was the father of our children, I don't know. I do know that in my heart that night, this would be the very last time I gave Tyrone this very important part or any other of myself. The bad in our marriage far outweighed the good. I remembered the legacy dad left me with years before. My big, pretty eyes had cried and cried and cried and I was through crying, over Tyrone anyway. Sometime later, as I recalled my past struggles with Tyrone to Evelyn, she said something that seemed to make all of my tears worthwhile. She said, "Sweetie, don't worry about your struggles or your tears. God has counted each tear you've ever cried and he's saved them all up. He's going to bless your every teardrop." That statement really made me feel like everything that I'd been through had not been in vain.

Chapter 20

The big day arrived without incidence. It was time for me to take my state boards so that I could finally work as a licensed nurse. Surprisingly enough, I wasn't very nervous. I saw this as an opportunity to finally set to work to achieve some of my goals. My car was not running well at all and thankfully, the school provided transportation for us to go to take the boards. It seemed that the results were back in a big hurry and I passed! I immediately set out to find work. I always dreamed of working in our hometown hospital and I wanted to specialize in Labor and Delivery. I always loved babies and I remember the special nurses that I was blessed to have with me during my labors and deliveries. I knew how thankful I was to have such sweet, compassionate and fully competent nurses with me and I desired to be just that kind of a nurse too. I wanted to be close to home given my car situation but I just didn't want to be in such close quarters with Tyrone. So for that reason I chose to work in North Carolina at a dialysis center. Dialysis was very interesting but the hours were very long, especially if one of the patients were in the hospital and I had to go to the hospital to dialyze them. I would find myself getting home some nights around nine o'clock. I totally missed spending time with my children, hearing how their days went, seeing what homework was done and how it was done. Even though Boobie and Cherylyn took excellent care of little busy Michael and John Lee, it wasn't their responsibility to have to care for their little brothers and themselves, it was my place to do it. Yet, I had to work so that I could take care of them. What a situation to be in. I worked there for six months, and then I came to the hospital at home and decided to put in an application for a job there. 'Forget Tyrone" is what I told myself. Sure enough, the director of nursing, who was a very lovely lady with a personality to match, hired me. I was given a job on Labor and Delivery as well. Although the only shift they had was night shift, I jumped at it. The pay was very low. I'll never forget how my salary was negotiated. The director of personnel, Ms. Wells, gave me a figure on the tiniest piece of paper. When I unfolded it, it had a minute figure on it. I accepted it because I would be home with my children during their most important times, after school in the evening hours. I could sleep during the day when John Lee slept because Michael was in kindergarten. Besides, my car was really acting up. So I weighed the bad, which was the salary, against the good, being home with my children. The good outweighed the bad.

One morning when I came home from work, I noticed something was wrong with John Lee. His little face was not looking right at all. His little chin had more than doubled in size and his left eyelid was almost closed. His left eye was rolling around without any control, or so it seemed. Thank God one of the very first things I did when I started working was to obtain health insurance for me and my children. I took him to the pediatrician who immediately sent us to an ophthalmologist in North Carolina. One look at John Lee and she called a very good hospital in Richmond, Va. Shortly after that, we were on our way. Prior to leaving, I had to go back home and ask dad if he would let Cherylyn and Michael stay with him until I came back from Richmond. I didn't want to leave them alone given the situation of the trailer. The weather was getting cold as well, and I didn't want to leave them alone with the kerosene heaters either. I wasn't sure how long I'd be gone but I knew that something was very wrong with John Lee. Dad agreed to keep them so off we drove to Richmond- Boobie, John Lee and me. I was praying all the way there that the car wouldn't put me down. There was this curve that you had to drive around as you approached the hospital. My car was in such ill repair that I would have to hold my door handle tightly as I drove around this curve, or the car door would fly open by itself. It's funny now as I reflect back on it but it wasn't funny then. Anyway, we made it there safely. As soon as we arrived, this team of Neurologists started doing all kinds of tests on John Lee. John Lee was so small. He was only three years old. As far as I was concerned, he was just a baby. I didn't understand the entire medical lingo either and this made me all the more worried. The test results would not be ready right away I was told. I was told that they would do a test on John Lee the next day where when injected with a silver solution, if his eyelid opened back to its normal appearance, they would then tell me what was wrong with him. Even though Boobie didn't want to leave us, I told him that I had to take him back home so that he could go to school. I took Boobie home that next morning. Dad agreed to keep him as well and I was very thankful for that. Before leaving home again, I went to the hospital and I told my director of nursing just what was going on. I felt bad to have to miss work after just getting hired. She totally understood and told me if I needed more time, just to let her know. I will always love her for her understanding and I will never forget her kindness.

So off I headed back to Richmond, my little raggedy car and all. By the time I arrived in John Lee's room, they had already done the test where they injected this silver dye-like substance in his vein. The doctor told me that my baby had Myasthenia Gravis. He went on to explain that this was a condition where the muscles used all the substances it needed for them to contract and expand early in the day and this was the cause for John Lee's eyelid drooping and his eyeball rolling around uncontrollably. He went on to say that this was diagnosed because when they injected the dye in John Lee's little vein, his eye lid automatically opened back to normal. He said, "This situation could worsen to the point where it could affect the diaphragm and he might be put on a respirator. This, of course, would hopefully reverse just as it came on and he would be off the respirator until the next episode." I can tell you now that I had never felt more alone in my entire life as I did now. I didn't know what to think or what to do. I just sat there by John Lee's bedside that night and prayed. I cried out to God and I told Him if He would just heal my little boy, I would live for Him and do everything I knew was right to do.

We stayed there for a week and in that week, somehow, I was able to eat properly, take John Lee down to the gift shop to buy him a stuffed animal and to the cafeteria where I bought him fruits. I cannot say where the money came from, except God. He supplied all my needs for that hospital stay. I was even able to buy this other little patient a stuffed animal. This little boy had taken to coming in John Lee's room. He would just sit there and talk to John Lee. John Lee would lay there and listen to this little boy and occasionally laugh with him. I appreciated this little boy of whom I don't even remember his name. Tyrone found out from whomever that John Lee was in the hospital. About the third or fourth day, he came to see John Lee. He only stayed a little while but I remember when Tyrone left, so did John Lee's fruit.

Chapter 21

As time went on John Lee's droopy eyelid stopped drooping. The only noticeable evidence of the Myasthenia Gravis was his left eye. It would still roll around uncontrollably at times. Nonetheless, he continued to grow like a little weed. He was in kindergarten the following year and he loved it. His teacher was a very sweet lady that had grown up with my sisters and me. She was a great teacher as well and John Lee loved her and loved to learn. The only thing John Lee did not like was getting on the school bus in the mornings. Each morning without fail, I would rush home from work to get the children ready for school. Each morning without fail, John Lee would scream and holler as soon as the bus pulled up. When I would try to pick him up to put him in the bus, he would grab hold of each side of the bus doors. As soon as I would pry his hands from the door, he would have his feet locked securely under the bus steps. This went on for some time. Finally, I told dad about it. He came to the trailer one evening and as soon as John Lee heard "Grandpa" coming, he ran and jumped in a pile of unfolded laundry I had in a chair in the bedroom. Dad came in and found where John Lee was hiding. He immediately pulled off that Zoro belt and started swinging at the pile of laundry. The next thing I remember is John Lee hollering and screaming and saying, "I'm gonna get on the bus, I'm gonna get on the bus." It sounded like John Lee had made a song out of "I'm gonna get on the bus." From that day until the day John Lee graduated high school, I never had any more problems with him getting on any school bus.

Boobie and Cherylyn did not give me any problems grow-ing up. Boobie remained a quiet, well-mannered child and he was very helpful with his brothers and sister. Cherylyn was very helpful too. She would get tired of going to mom's house and putting her on the bedside commode every night. She was just plain ole tired of going down to mom's house every night anyway. She wanted to play and spend time with her friends but she had to help out with mom. She knew that if she re-fused, dad would give her a beating. Michael was as busy as he could be in school and out of school. At home, he would find all kinds of mischief to get into. Even as a baby, about eleven months old or so, he threw his bottle out of the car win-dow as we were riding down the street. I pulled over at the gas station to try to retrieve his bottle and he jumped head first out of the car window. He never even cried. He had this huge knot on his forehead but he went right along as though nothing was wrong. On another occasion, he burned his hand on dad's wood stove in the kitchen. No one knew what he had done until we noticed his skin bubbling up on his little hand. I was scared silly but Michael was still running around playing. As his hand was healing and forming a scab, he would bite it off each time. This made my skin crawl to see him do that. I finally tied a piece of cloth around his hand so he couldn't get to it and it finally healed. I took him to the emergency room on so many occasions; I think the nurses actually suspected me of abusing him after a while.

I never knew when Michael was sick because he never slowed down being busy. On one occassion though, he was very quiet. He was about four years old. He wouldn't eat either so I knew something was wrong. Because Tyrone had never purchased health insurance for us, when I took Michael to the doctor, they acted as though they really didn't want to see us. The care was minimal and abrupt and I would leave with Michael still feeling bad. This went on for about a month. Then I noticed that Michael couldn't breathe well. A wonderful Pediatrician named Dr. Beshai, who I will never forget in my life, was who I had the pleasure to meet on this particular visit. He saw Michael and was genuinely concerned about him. He had the most wonderful bedside mannerism I had ever seen in any doctor. He encouraged me not to worry about anything. As it turned out, Michael had obstructive tonsillitis. My health insurance had not kicked in yet, but Dr. Beshai admitted Michael to the hospital anyway. He then consulted for Michael to go to Petersburg to see a doctor there to prepare for a tonsillectomy. On the day of the surgery, there we were-me, Boobie, and Michael lying in the back seat of my old, trusty car. Boobie was always my little man and he'd stick right by my side through whatever. The surgery went on without any problems and I remember driving back home and looking back frequently to watch Michael lying there quietly. This was a rare occasion indeed.

Michael was very smart in school and he would finish his school work fast and then disrupt the class being a clown with the remainder of his time. He was always a good-natured, happy person but he was very hyperactive as well. I remember in the second grade, he was not permitted to go on any field trips unless I accompanied him. Needless to say, I went on an awful lot of field trips. When I would tell dad how he behaved in school, he would give Michael a beating as well. Dad never missed an opportunity to give anyone a beating. He thought beating you was the answer to world hunger, world peace and everything else. After dad would get a hold of Michael, Michael would fall asleep. I guess that was his defense mechanism. I had to rely on dad to be a father figure to my children because I knew that they desperately needed a father figure. I don't believe that giving those beatings was the cure for everything though.

I remember when Michael was in the third grade, his teacher held a conference with me. She told me that I should take him to a child psychologist to have him evaluated. At first I was very upset with her. I thought she was insinuating that my child was crazy or something. After much thought, I scheduled an appointment with a child psychologist. At the appointment the psychologist asked me and Michael a lot of questions. Then in reading her summary, it seemed that she had taken down everything we said and put it on paper. I really didn't see where that was any help. She then wrote a prescription to have Michael take a drug called Ritalin. When I researched this drug, I found out it was simply Speed. It was supposed to have the opposite affect on children as adults. It was supposed to slow children down and help them to focus. I didn't give it to Michael right away though. It took me almost three years before I gave in to this therapy.

Almost every night, I would pray that God would send me a good husband for myself and a good father for my children. I messed around with some guys but I found that I lost interest in them very quickly. They just were not what I was looking for. I wasn't sure exactly what I was looking for myself but

I knew I didn't want another Tyrone. I would call Martha's house, infrequently now, to try to ask Tyrone to spend time with his children. I didn't think it was my place to have to beg and plead with a man to take an interest in his own children. Even though we didn't make it, what did that have to do with the children? I knew the children were hurting as well from not having Tyrone show any interest in them whatsoever. I especially could see how Michael was hurting from the lack of having his father's love. I think some of his hyperactivity was a form of acting out to gain attention. Now, as I look back on things, I think Michael was an angry and confused little boy on the inside as well. No matter how much love and attention I gave him, it could not take the place of a bond that only a father has with his son. I was at a loss for what to do to comfort him emotionally. The guys that I would spend time with only seemed to want to spend time with me; they didn't seem too interested in my children. This caused me to loose interest in them with the quickness!

One day almost a year after John Lee's hospital bout, Evelyn called me. She said, "Cheryl, I had to call you because the Lord told me to tell you this. I don't know what you promised Him when John Lee was sick, but He told me to tell you that whatever it is you promised Him, you have to do it." Well, I was awestruck to say the least. No one, except me and God knew what I promised Him in that hospital room that night when I was at my wit's end. I had totally forgotten what I promised God until that day when Evelyn brought it all back to mind. Still, I went on, doing my thing. I wasn't doing anything wrong to anyone but I had not kept my promise to do God's will either. Here I was, seeing men, sleeping with some of them, in my search for the perfect husband and father. Evelyn was always a very scary person to me when she did things like that. She was a lot like mom in her ability to tell you things that could only come from a higher power. I dreaded her phone calls for a while after that.

Chapter 22

Tyrone decided to move away again. Since he rarely interacted with his children, his move was no big loss. The only thing is that when he left, so did the child support check. I worked with his sister Queeta in the labor and delivery department. We were never close because I felt she was always jealous of the relationship I had with Martha. Whenever Martha would give one of the children something, anything, Queeta would become very upset. For this reason, I was never interested in forming with her what I envisioned a sister-n-law bond should be. At work, whenever I would ask her if she knew where Tyrone was, she would always reply, "Cheryl, I don't know where he is." I would tell her that I really needed to contact him so that I could set up the support for the children. It always amazed me that even though she never knew where he was, she would tell me from time to time that "Tyrone called the other day. He says he's doing fine." After a while, I stopped inquiring about him altogether. I had adopted the same mindset about my children that dad had about mom. I would do the very best that I could for them if I fell off of my feet trying. Instead of having a pity party, I went to a lawyer and filed for divorce.

That winter, my trusty little raggedy car stopped working altogether. I would put it in the shop only to be patched up and returned to me with the same problems happening again within a few weeks time. Finally, I just let the wrecker tow it away. I was still working midnights so about ten o'clock at nights; I would kiss each of my children good night and start out walking to work. I would walk back home in the mornings and surprisingly, I would make it home before it was time to get the children on the bus. There was this lady I worked with that worked midnights with me. I nicknamed her Vee. She learned that I was walking back and forth to work every night and she said, "Cheryl, since I pass right by you going to work, I'll stop and pick you up and drop you off in the mornings. I could hardly hold back the tears of joy and appreciation. So that is what Vee did. I thank God for Vee and I'll always love her and will never forget her for this and the many acts of love and kindness that she showed me through the years. She had a sense of humor out of this world and she could make me fall out laughing at her even on my worst day.

Money was really a huge issue. It seemed there was never enough money to provide enough food, clothes, school supplies and school associated needs in general, etc. for four children and myself. The trailer continued to fall apart as well. Where there had only been a hole in the kitchen floor, now there was a hole right at the front door entrance, a hole in the hallway and holes in the entrances to both bathrooms. The front door would not close well or lock either. I would be ashamed for my sisters or my children's friends to come to visit because of the appearance of our trailer. There was also an issue with keeping my children warm, especially with having to leave them at night when the temperatures would be at their lowest. We did have the two kerosene heaters but with the draftiness of the trailer because of the holes, it would still be cool in the trailer. Before leaving for work, I would cover the children with all of the blankets that I had, then I would pile coats on top of them. I couldn't really secure them inside because of the door that wouldn't lock and this would really worry me. To comfort myself, I would pray each and every night before leaving for work and ask God to protect them and to keep them from all hurt, harm and danger. Then I would leave for work with a sense of comfort. I would confide in Doll about all of my struggles. She would encourage me to move to Georgia where she was. She would tell me, "Girl, you can make it so much better here than in that little small town where opportunity for growth is rare. People won't be all up in your business here either." Even though all of this sounded good, I could not bring myself to leave mom when she really needed me.

I will always be grateful for Ms. Ruby and her little store that was right beside our trailer. Whenever the food and kerosene was low, I could always count on her. I would send Boobie over with a note and she would fill the order for us. She would allow me to charge these items until I got paid. On some occasions I would have run my bill up to a point where I knew I wouldn't be able to pay the trailer payment and other bills if I continued to charge from her. On some of those occasions, as much as I hated to, I would ask dad if he would loan me enough money to buy some kerosene for the heaters until my next 2 paydays. After a big lecture on how I should learn to budget my money and take care of my own children, he would finally give me about ten dollars. Ten dollars certainly would not buy much kerosene or anything else even back in those days but I would take it anyway and thank him

for his help. I would still go to help out with mom and him
and I didn't mind doing whatever I could for them. I didn't
enjoy going down to their house though because I did resent
dad for being so blind to my needs when he clearly saw I was
struggling by myself to take care of my children. I thought,
"How do I budget when I don't even make enough money to
budget?" I got so tired of dad fussing about everything that
the children and I did or how we did it, instead of being ap-
preciative. Dad would have no problem coming to pick us up
to carry us to his house to prepare mom for bed and help him
out with whatever he needed done, yet, he would have a problem when I would ask him to carry me to the grocery store. I
remember on one occasion, Cherylyn and I were walking back
home from downtown. We had been to the grocery store and
we each had lots of bags to carry. As we were walking we spotted dad driving up the street toward us. Cherylyn and I were
so happy because we were so tired. We knew that dad would
see us and take us home. Well, I don't know whether or not
he saw us or heard us because we were hollering at him. He
never looked around at us. Tired and all, we made it home
with the bags anyway. I had a real problem with him getting
up to preach and teach and tell of God's love but not show that
same love at home. He would stand in the pulpit and flash
the prettiest smile down at the children and I and this would
really make me literally sick. I really had to swallow a lot of
the resentment I felt for dad so that I could go to help mom.
If it had not been for my unyielding love for mom, I probably
would not have continued to go. After all, she had shown me
unconditional love all of my life. I made up my mind that I
would not ask dad for anything else. The children and I would
just do the best we could and do without if need be. So where I
would ask him to take me to the grocery store, Cherylyn and I

would walk downtown to the grocery store and push the groceries back in the cart or carry them back, whichever. I would continue to cover my children with coats, clothing or whatever else at nights so as to have peace of mind that they would be warm enough. Spring would come soon.

Chapter 23

Indeed, spring did come and with it came a new sense of accomplishing new goals for myself. The lawyer needed Tyrone to come into the office to sign the paperwork to have the divorce finalized. I told Queeta this and even though she didn't have a clue as to where he was, sure enough, he showed up at the lawyer's office right on schedule. He signed the paperwork and so the divorce was final. Even though the court ordered child support was included in the divorce decree, Tyrone never adhered to it. Nonetheless, I was able to pay for the divorce with my income tax refund for that year. About 10 years ago, I checked to see just how much he was delinquent in child support payments. The figure then was approximately $256,000. At any rate, I could now put this chapter of Tyrone far behind me.

I needed a car so badly. I didn't know how I could pay for one but I went out on faith anyway. As it turned out, I was blessed with a very nice car that very day. Boobie was just starting to learn to drive too. He had his learner's permit and he enjoyed driving. It did my heart good to see the children enjoying having a car. I no longer had to depend on anyone to take us anywhere and what a relief that was in itself. Would you believe that dad actually asked me to drive my car to North Carolina to one of the church functions? Well, I let him. He gladly left me the keys to his car that day. Then, he locked the keys up in my new car and I ended up going to North Carolina to take him my extra keys. There was no shame to Dad's game!

There was a prison facility that was to open soon. It was about seven miles from my house. I would hear some of the nurses talking about it. They would say that the pay was great as were the hours. I loved labor and delivery. I worked with the greatest bunch of women that anyone could ever hope for. I loved providing professional, compassionate care to my laboring patients, my ante partum patients, and I loved the babies. I prided myself on being the very best nurse that I could be and each morning that I left work, I left with a sense of satisfaction that I had provided the very best care that I could. Yet, the salary was a definite issue. I was tired of working nights too. I wanted to be at work when my children were at school, and be at home with them when they were at home. I always believed that children needed their parents when they were small for sure, but they needed their parents even more as they grew older. I thought also that if I should take this job at the prison, I wouldn't be so tired in the evenings after getting mom's needs taken care of, only to come home to lay down for a few hours before going to work. It seemed like the pros, again, outweighed the cons. So, off I went to apply for a job. I was given a job there and was delighted to find that I would be making $4.00 more an hour and would be given the morning shift. "How very good God is" is all I could think as I drove back home to tell the children of our newest blessing.

As much as I hated to, I resigned from the hospital and left for my very new adventure in the prison environment.

What an adventure it was. Nursing in the prison system was totally different from the nursing in which I had been accustomed. In orientation, we were taught that the people in the infirmaries and buildings were to be referred to as inmates, not patients. This took some getting used to for me. I was accustomed to referring to my patients as my patients. I was surprised by the general consensus that "inmates are nothing more than inmates. They are slick and con artists and must be thought of in this way, always." I was not used to this way of thinking, stereotyping everyone to be in one class because they were incarcerated. Nonetheless, I stayed there. The money was a huge, much needed blessing and I wasn't going to let any terminology or ways of thinking block my blessings. I just continued to be the kind of nurse I'd always been- caring, compassionate and sensitive to the needs of other people, whether they were inmates or free. I realized that inmates were real people with real illnesses, just as anyone else. I never wanted to loose sight of the fact that this could be me, or one of my children in this situation. I certainly wouldn't want any care withheld from one of us if the shoe were on the other foot. It was true that a lot of them did pretend to have one complaint or another. I would just ignore them and deal with those that had real, documented complaints. For me, it wasn't hard at all to discern which complaints were real and which were not.

With the increased salary and new schedule, I was able to enroll Michael and John Lee in sports. They played tee ball and thoroughly enjoyed it. Sports proved to be especially good for Michael. He was given the opportunity to channel all that extra energy into something positive. I also enrolled Cherylyn in the girl's softball program. I don't believe she was

ever seriously interested though. Her position was in the out-
field. When a ball came her way, she'd just stand there with
her gloved hand on her hip and watch as the ball landed. She
would occasionally duck if it seemed the ball was heading
right for her. Boobie didn't really want to play baseball. He
liked football more, so when summertime came, that is what I
would enroll him in.

I was now seriously envisioning a new home, a real house
for my children. I was able to pay off the bills that Tyrone
left me with along with my present ones as well. This new
schedule was working great. I was at work when the children
were in school. I could take the time off that I needed to go
to school for programs and any other school event that required my presence. I would be late sometimes and for John
Lee, this would be a disaster when he would look around and
not see my face. When I would arrive at the school, he would
be screaming and crying to the top of his lungs. Some of the
teachers and other parents would be trying to comfort him,
all to no avail. As soon as he saw me, he would run to me and
give me a big hug and all would be well in his little world
again. I was able to thoroughly enjoy the evenings with the
children and they enjoyed having me at home and not being tired or groggy from working nights. I was able to spend
quality time with them and with mom. I wasn't tired anymore
when I helped dad out with her. I could even better tolerate
dad's lecturing, fussing and complaining. I actually enjoyed
being around dad sometimes. He would prepare a great meal
some evenings and invite the children and me to eat with him
and mom. Dad was a great cook and on those occasions when
he wasn't complaining, he was actually quite enjoyable to be
around and to listen to. Dad was a man of great wisdom as
well and I learned quite a lot from listening to him.

Chapter 24

On some days, I would volunteer to work in the buildings where the inmates were actually housed as opposed to the infirmary. I've always been the adventurous type and I've always wanted to see how different areas of my workplace operated. I felt that learning different types of skills made me all the more marketable. As opposed to the infirmary where there were a lot of very chronically ill patients, working in the buildings was different. There was not a lot of hard, physical work involved. This environment consisted basically of preparing medicines, basically pills and insulin for the men who were on prescribed medications. These men would come to the pill window and we would issue these medicines to them. We would also go inside the pods of the prison and issue medications to those men who were in segregation and could not come out to the pill window to get their meds. I met a nice, crazy kind of nurse working the buildings. Her name was Ms. Robbins. She was a good nurse and I could tell she'd worked in the prison system for a while because she had this kind of rapport with the men. She was straight up with them and them with her, yet they seemed to have a mutual respect for each other. She also had a great sense of humor and it seemed the shift went by quickly when we worked together. Whenever overtime was available, I would work it when the children didn't have any planned activities. The money was very good and I could see my future home clearly now.

One day Ms. Robbins says to me, "I've got somebody I want you to meet." I said, "What do you mean meet?" She says, "Just what I said. His name is Tobias and he's a very nice guy. He's lonesome and needs to meet someone." I fired right back at her, "I didn't come here to meet anyone; I came here to work." Nothing more was said about that issue. Then, a few weeks later, Ms. Robbins called me to the pill window. She said, "Cheryl, I have someone for you to meet." When I walked over to the pill window, standing there was this man who was staring at me as awkwardly as I must have been staring at him. He looked just as uninterested as I must have. We spoke and shared some idle talk and shortly after that, he went back to where he had come from and I continued my work of getting the medicines together for the next pill call. I didn't see him again for a couple weeks. Then one day, he came to the pill window again. This time, when I was summoned by Ms. Robbins to come to the window, there stood Tobias. I said hello and that started a long conversation. This man was talking non-stop and his conversation was a very intense one to put it mildly. In his talking, I noticed that this guy was extremely intelligent and well versed and well learned in a lot of areas. Some of the things he said were totally over my head and I'd always prided myself on being very smart and very intelligent as well. We talked my entire break period; I mostly listened. Tobias seemed to have had this conversation pent up inside of him for years at the rate he was talking. I couldn't help but to notice his eyes as he spoke. He had the most beautiful, dark, serious eyes I had ever seen. As he walked away from the pill window, I noticed his butt. He had the nicest butt I had ever seen on any man before in my life as well. I wondered to myself as I watched him walk away, "How in the world did I miss seeing those sexy, dark, serious eyes and that butt the first time I met him?" Needless to say, I found myself mesmerized by his high level of intelligence, his eyes, and yes, his butt.

Tobias and I started writing each other. I had to use one of my cousin's addresses so as not to bring attention to me or him. In writing, I learned that he had been in prison for two years already. I also learned that this was his second time being incarcerated. As a teenager, he ran on the streets of D.C. and he ran with the wrong crowds as well. This helped to land him in prison the first time. He said that when he was paroled the first time, he lived with his father and step-mother until something happened that caused him to be put out of their home. Then he went to live with his mother and step-father and because their home was so far out from everything, this was not a workable set up either. He then came to live with his grandmother and worked as a butcher, then as a barber. He said he felt that he didn't have the family support that he needed to be as productive as he should have been and he gradually drifted back out in the streets. He told me he had 2 brothers and a sister but he had not heard anything from them since this incarceration. He also told me that his parents were dead. I thought, "What a horrible situation to be in." I told him some things about my life too. I told him that I had four children of whom I adored. I let him know that they were my life. I told him a little about my rocky 12 year marriage and ultimate divorce. I told him how Tyrone would fight me whenever he felt like it and Tobias became very angry. He told me "Don't you ever let no man put his hands on you, ever again!" As we continued to converse, I found myself drawn to this man more and more. Even though I didn't come to the prison to find a pen pal, friend, husband, or anything else but a paycheck, things were certainly turning around rapidly.

Tyrone was back in town at Martha's or somewhere over that way. Anyway, one summer evening at work, I received a telephone call from him. He said, "Cheryl, we need to get back together for the kids." I had never cursed at Tyrone before, but today was a very different day. I had never really cursed at all until I started working at the prison. In that environment, I heard cursing day in and day out, from everybody! Anyway, I cursed Tyrone out that day. I told him, "Why do you think I divorced you if I wanted to stay with you," but with more choice words. Then I slammed the telephone down and went back to work. I would never have gone back to him whether I had met Tobias or not. I had become friends with a girl that I'd known all my life but not really gotten to know as a child growing up. I called her Dale. I found her now to be a very good friend with a very entertaining sense of humor. I could always confide in her. Her mother lived next door to Martha and I'm sure her mom told Martha about Tobias and me. The rest is history.

As I observed Tobias more and more, I noticed that he was a real rough neck. He stood up to whomever, whenever, whether they were other inmates, officers, the major, the warden, whoever and he was an expert on voicing his grievances on paper. It seemed that when Tobias felt he was right about something, he would carry it to the very top. He did not complain to get attention as I noticed some of the other men did. If he didn't mean it, he didn't say it. If he meant it, he said it. He was very blunt in conversation, he would say whatever it

was on his mind to say and he didn't try to fix his conversation
beforehand so that it wouldn't come out as offensive. He'd just
say exactly what was on his mind and if it hurt your feelings,
oh well. About a month after we begin seriously talking and
writing, he asked me to marry him. Well, I was totally floored.
I didn't know what to think or to say, so I didn't say anything
right away. I went home and discussed this with my little person Boobie. He was always my strength and even though he
was a teenager, I valued his opinions on a lot of things. Boobie
said, "Mom, if you want to marry him, I think you should wait
until he gets out, and then see if you want to marry him." I listened to him and pondered his advice. I finally found enough
courage to discuss Tobias with dad. Well dad was too through
with me when I told him I wanted to marry an inmate. He
strongly discouraged it and said he didn't approve and would
never approve this marriage. I was always the type of person
to value advice, but I would end up doing whatever it was
that I felt was best for me in the end. I was never a pretentious
person either, so it was clear to my co-workers that I was falling in love with an inmate, they just didn't know who, that
is, besides Ms. Robbins. So after six months of working in the
prison environment, I gave my two-week resignation. I went
back to the hospital and talked with the nursing director. She
was as sweet and understanding as she'd always been and she
said she would be very glad to have me back. She told me that
she'd always valued my work as a nurse and I could work
in OB/GYN again. When she told me this, it brought to mind
something dad always told us. He said, "Your gift will make
room for you." I felt very proud that I had put my energies
into being the very best nurse that I could be. There were no
day positions open so I would have to work nights again. I
was also offered to work this new shift that was developed

which was working on weekends only, for 36 hours and being paid for 40 hours. I jumped at the chance.

My co-workers at the prison were very nice to me, as well as understanding. They gave me a very nice going away party and lots of well wishes. I love and appreciate them for their kindness even now. So here I was, all set for a new adventure indeed. I thought to myself, "Lord, I know I've been praying and asking for a good husband and a good father for my children but I didn't expect to find one in prison." I never doubted my decision to work at the prison, to become friends with Tobias once I decided to stop and talk to him and get to know some things about him, or to resign. This gave me peace of mind and an inner comfort that this was indeed God working in my life yet again.

I was very surprised to learn that even though Tobias had two brothers and a sister, he had not even submitted a visitor's list since he had been in prison. I found this very odd. When I asked him about that, he said he never saw the need to have one because he felt his family wasn't close to him. He said that even though he'd written to them, they never wrote back so he found it useless to continue to communicate by himself. He also told me that his parents were very much alive. He originally told me that they were dead. He said he told me they were dead because they were dead to him in spirit. He said thinking of them as being dead made it easier for him to deal with receiving no communication from them. He said that because of a misunderstanding between him and his "Pops", he hadn't talked to his dad in years. I told him that dead or alive, I would have to meet his mother in the visiting room before I would marry him. I always felt that one could tell what type of man he really was by seeing how he interacted with his mother. If he disrespected his mother, then I knew that I would not marry him because he would certainly disrespect me. I learned this from watching Tyrone interact with Martha. He thought nothing of disrespecting her, especially when she didn't give in to his childish whims. Anyway, Tobias agreed to our meeting. He gave me his mother's address and telephone number and I immediately went about setting up our first meeting.

Chapter 25

Mother, as she asked that I call her, was very pleasant to talk with. I told her why I needed to meet her and she gave me her word that she would come down to visit Tobias and meet me. She then gave me a little lecture on how I should really think about what I was doing. She went on to say that I was so young and was I really willing to put my life on hold to wait for Tobias? She reminded me that Tobias was in no position to contribute anything financially to a family right now and that she wanted me to think everything over before I made any firm decision to marry Tobias. We scheduled a weekend to meet at the prison. Later when Mother and I were reminiscing about our initial conversation about me marrying her son she said, "Cheryl, I was thinking while reading the letter that you wrote me telling me you wanted to marry Tobias that you were some crazy person. Then, as I continued to read on, I said, this is a very intelligent person writing this letter. Then I thought, she just got somebody to write this for her. Then I thought, this must be some little skeezer or some ugly heifer with soup coolers that hang down to her chin. Something must be wrong with her for her to want to marry an inmate. She must be crazy as hell! Then, when I met you, you were such an attractive, innovative, intelligent woman and I felt badly because I didn't want you to put your life on hold. I didn't want Tobias to hurt you or you him. Anyway, I thank God for your presence in all of our lives." I rolled with laughter at this very funny, very serious woman as she told me what she was really thinking initially.

It was my first trip to the prison as a visitor. As I entered the doors, I felt like I had just escaped from a prison or had grown horns or something. I was getting stares and glares and I felt very uncomfortable initially. Then a saying that mom used from time to time came to mind; "You run your mouth, I'll run my business." With that thought in mind, I moved right along. As I entered the visiting room and after finding a table, I began to relax. There were a lot of the officers that did not hide their dislike in my seeing an inmate. I always wondered why they had so much interest in my life. I never noticed it before. These people didn't even know me. If they were to be asked in all honesty what Cheryl ever did to them to harm them or disrespect them, if they were to answer honestly, they would say, "She never did us any harm or bothered any one of us." So, with this reassurance in mind, I just sat there at that table and waited nervously for Tobias to come out. Finally, I spotted him at the front door of the entrance. He eventually came into the visiting room. I was nervous then for real! He came over and I stood to greet him. He hugged me and kissed me and I knew then that whatever anyone else thought didn't even matter. I wasn't doing anything to hurt anybody so I would not feel condemned about anything. We had a really nice visit. We held hands throughout the visit as we listened to each other talk about ourselves, our aspirations, our views, our beliefs, our dislikes, etc. We went to the vending machines and Tobias really enjoyed the foods. I enjoyed watching him eat. When the visit was over, we kissed passionately and my heart skipped a few beats I'm sure. This felt so right, so good. As I left the prison, I kept thinking, "I can't wait till tomorrow!" The visit the next day was just as good. I knew that I could love this man for the rest of my life. Although he was very, very male, brash, hardcore, rough neck; he was also very intelligent, interesting, sexy, handsome, sensitive, romantic, gentle, naughty, and he appealed to all of my senses. It was imperative that he meet the children so we decided that, the next weekend, we all would visit. I left him feeling very excited in my spirit.

Later that evening, I discussed Tobias with the children. I told him that mommy was going to marry him only if they approved after meeting him. John Lee and Michael were so young. I'm not sure whether or not they fully understood but everyone was in agreement just the same. Saturday came quickly and we all went to visit Tobias. I had talked to the children to prepare them for what to expect but I still think they were a little amazed nonetheless. It was all new to them to get frisked, take their shoes off and have someone check them out from head to toe. After going through the ritual of waiting for steel doors to slide open and slam shut behind us, we finally reached the visiting room. After waiting for a while, Tobias finally came out. As he approached the table, he kissed and hugged me. Then he hugged each one of the boys and hugged and kissed Cherylyn. He bonded with each of them instantly, all four of them. He wanted to know their interests, dislikes and he shared some of his experiences and poor choices with them. He never missed an opportunity to tell them that this environment was not one that they would want to be in. The

children bonded with him as well. John Lee was a little shy.
He was my baby and because of his illness, I had paid special
attention to him. I guess, in other words, I had spoiled him
along the way. Anyway, we all had a nice visit and the children
approved of him, even Boobie.

As the weekend visits went along, there was this lady that
came to visit her brother-n-law. She would come with her sister. Both she and her sister were very attractive women and
they wore very pretty clothes to further accentuate their nice
figures. Anyway, Renita, as I later learned was her name, was
very interested in Tobias. I could, as can any woman or man
for that matter, tell when someone else has an interest in their
interest. I think Tobias was quite flattered by her obvious interest. I felt that he was curious about her as well. Where he
would sit down at our table and talk nonstop, I noticed that
whenever Renita entered the visiting room, he would be at a
momentary loss for words. She would look around the room
until she saw Tobias there as well. After she spotted Tobias,
she would produce the widest, prettiest smile, for him I suppose. They both would make eye contact and I could feel their
chemistries probably as much as they could. Anyway, when
Renita would be in the visiting room, Tobias would become
very restless acting. He would walk, very briskly around the
visiting room, from one person's table to another, telling them
something, anything I suppose. When the families got back
on the bus, or trolley, to go back to the main entrance, Renita
would just sit there and discretely watch me and the children.
I noticed her sitting there watching me but I never said anything to her. A couple months before our proposed marriage
I asked Tobias, "Are you sure you want to marry me? I can
feel chemistry between you and Renita and I don't want to
get married if you're not sure I'm the one that you want to be

with." Tobias replied, "Sweetheart, I'm sitting here with you and the children aren't I? I'm right where I want to be. I talked with Renita on the telephone and she wouldn't be what I am looking for in a wife." I was surprised that he had talked to her but I was relieved to know that he had done so. I was not willing to place my heart in harms way any more and I loved Tobias enough to want to see him happy with whomever he chose to be with. As time went on, the wide, pretty smiles that had been on Renita's face when she entered the visiting room were now just plain ole grimaces, especially when she looked at me and Tobias. This made me feel much better! Seeing her like that actually put a big ole pretty smile on my face. She finally stopped coming altogether.

The weekend to meet Mother finally came. I was nervous but I was more excited for Tobias than I was nervous. He hadn't seen his mother in a few years and I hoped that he would be able to reconcile whatever differences with his mother so that he would feel better. I was sitting in the waiting area. This was a huge facility so you would have to catch a trolley to the different buildings. I was just sitting there when I noticed a lady sitting down from me. As I took in her features, I noticed that she had the same skin complexion as Tobias. The eyes and smile were the same too. She was a very attractive lady and Tobias looked just like her. I walked over to her and said, "Hi, you must be Tobias' mother because he looks just like you." She smiled and we hugged as she said, "You must be Cheryl." We went down to the visiting room together and I felt relaxed as we talked. We sat down at one of the tables and waited for Tobias to come in. I was very anxious to see just how he would react to seeing his mother after such a long time. He came over to the table and she stood to greet him. He just hugged her and hugged her and hugged her. She was crying and I just sat there feeling all mushy inside. After what seemed quite a few minutes, Tobias sat down and kissed and hugged me. He sat between Mother and me so we all were able to talk as he held my hand firmly in his. Then Mother started to question him as to why he wanted to marry me. I'll never forget his response. He looked at Mother squarely, eye to eye and said, "Because I love her." After a few moments of quiet thought, Mother gave us her blessings. It was a really nice visit. I enjoyed watching Tobias interact with Mother. He was as gentle as a lamb with her and I could tell he loved her dearly. I couldn't help but thank God for this man. After our visit, Mother, her girlfriend that had rode down with her, and I went out to this nice little restaurant and enjoyed a great dinner. As I thanked Mother and said my good byes, I told her that it had been very good to meet her and that I looked forward to seeing her again soon. I told her I would keep her informed of the wedding plans.

Chapter 26

Settling back into the routine of working nights was easy. I worked with Vee again and a very sweet nurse that I nicknamed AJ. Everything was falling right into place. Being able to spend all week with the children was wonderful. I could check on mom during the week with no problems too. Tyrone had gotten his old job back at the hospital and he was working nights as well. He went out of his way to stay out of my way so all went well indeed. Sometimes, when walking down the hallways at night, Tyrone would bump into me as if the hallways weren't large enough for both of us to pass without touching. Anyway, I just ignored him. I was busy planning my wedding together with Dale's assistance. Even though I had come under a lot of scrutiny with my decision to marry an inmate, Dale still stayed in my corner. Her little girl was going to be my little flower girl. That really meant a lot to me. I didn't have the money for the wedding necessities, so I had to rely on my tax returns. Tobias and I had discussed a wedding date and we decided on February 14th. What more fitting a day than Valentine's Day? I remember actually measuring Tobias with a measuring tape that we measured the babies with at birth, in the visiting room for his tuxedo. I did a pretty good job too, considering what I was working with. The income tax return came right on time, about 2 weeks before the BIG day, so I was able to pick up the rings, the tuxes, shoes, Cherylyn's dress and accessories, and my gown, shoes and head piece. I believed God was really working everything out. No one could convince me otherwise.

Sitting in the visiting room just a week before our wedding day, I kept asking Tobias if he were nervous. He always denied being nervous. He didn't seem nervous. I sure was! I remember having to go through all the departmental procedures before we could get married. I, of course, had to provide Tobias with a copy of my divorce papers. Then he had to write to the Warden, I believe, for permission to marry and to okay the proposed date. Then, I had to come up to the prison on a weekday. I was taken to this little room where Tobias came inside shortly after. He sat down beside me and we kissed. We talked and were totally absorbed in each other when this person came into the room and asked us questions. I remember one specific question particularly. It was, "How many times have you been married." Tobias wrote and replied simultaneously, "It's my first and last." He had this way of making me melt on the inside without even trying to.

It was the morning of the big day. I was very nervous, but in a good kind of way, you know? I had decided to cut my hair and I'm glad I did. It looked very nice. Boobie was walking me down the isle, giving his mama away to this man, so I rented him a very nice black and burgundy tux. Cherylyn was my little maid of honor and I bought her a very nice cream-colored, lacy dress with shoes to match. Michael and John Lee had on their little suits and they looked so cute. I wore a lacy, burgundy colored gown with head piece to match. My shoes were burgundy as well. I looked pretty good. My next door neighbor, Bea, came along with me. She was a very nice neighbor and friend and I was honored to have her present on my big day. Before going to the prison, I had to stop and pick up Dale's daughter and my wedding party would then be complete. Bea later told me that when I drove up to Dale's mother's house, she saw Martha and maybe Tyrone peeking out of the window. It really didn't matter one way or the other. When we arrived at the prison, there was Mother and her husband, Jamie already there and waiting. I had not met Jamie before but what a really nice guy he was. He was such a pleasant fellow and he seemed to be naturally happy and jolly. I liked him immediately. I hugged him and Mother. I told them I was so glad they could come and I sincerely was. Jamie had agreed to be Tobias' best man and I thought that was very nice of him to do it. There was also another of my good friends there to support me. Her name was Lydia. She had just gotten married there shortly before. I gave Tobias's tux, shoes, and socks to an officer so that they could check it and take it to Tobias. I was hoping that the tux fit given my measuring expertise, or should I say, inexpertise. After completing all the standard procedures of getting through the gates, we boarded the trolley car. When we arrived at the visiting room door, I really did get those butterflies and nervous jitters. Lydia did a great job coordinating the wedding and she made sure everyone was where they were supposed to be. Boobie and I waited in the entrance area while everyone was awaiting my arrival. I kept asking Boobie, "Do I look alright, are you sure?" I'm sure he was just about ready to duct tape my mouth if he'd had the duct tape but he remained his patient and calm self and reassured me each time I would ask him the same thing. Finally, it was time for me to "walk down the aisle" to receive my husband. As I came closer to the chapel area, I could not help but to stare at Tobias. He was standing there with his arms in front of him, one hand crossed over the other, watching me as I came toward him. He stood there looking extremely handsome. He had a fresh haircut; his skin was glowing, the tux, cream-colored with a burgundy tie and cumber bun fit very nicely, burgundy socks and shoes; he looked GOOD! As I approached Tobias, he immediately took my hand in his. Anyway, after the minister asked who was giving me to Tobias, and Boobie said that he was, the ceremony was underway. I looked to my left where there was a window and there I saw Ms. Robbins standing there smiling. I smiled back at her. The ceremony didn't take very long and after placing the rings on each other's fingers and the matrimonial kiss, it was done, we were now man and wife. We were then allowed to go inside the visiting room for about two hours or so. In talking with Lydia and another lady that I had met from visiting, they were given time alone with their husbands. Tobias and I were hoping that we would be given this opportunity as well, but we weren't. Given how I had been silently, and sometimes not so silently ridiculed almost every time I visited Tobias, I really wasn't surprised. I don't think he was either. We had a nice time visiting with family and friends, sharing a cheeseburger since I couldn't bring in a cake and just enjoying being together anyway. Tobias was allowed to bring in a CD and player. We danced to a song he had chosen beforehand, Highway to Heaven by the O'Jays and what a great choice it was. After our time together was over, I felt so sad that I had to leave him there and that I would be all alone on my wedding night, again. We kissed goodbye and told each other that we would see the other on tomorrow. As I rode away on the trolley, he and some of his well-wishers were standing out on the yard waving at us. Tobias was shouting, "I love you!"

That night, while lying in bed, I kept thinking how very much I missed Tobias. I hugged my pillow as I thought about him and what he was doing, thinking, feeling at this very moment. Even though I felt a huge longing and emptiness in my heart, I also felt Tobias' love and longing for me and those feelings encompassed my dreams that night.

True to our plans, we visited the next morning as man and wife. It felt really good. We had already discussed our desires to have more children. I personally always wanted six and when I would tell people this the general response would be, "Girl, are you crazy?" Tobias did not have any children and I knew he really loved and wanted children of his own, as well as the four that I brought into the marriage with me. As I said before, Tobias was a very intelligent, very innovative man. He was adamant about having a child of his own and once he set his mind to it, nobody could talk him out of it. There were no obstacles too high or too low for him. There were quite a few times in the visiting room that Tobias literally scared me to death in his quest to have a child. Even though I was scared silly, Tobias' adventurous side always appealed to me and replaced all fear that I felt; well most of it anyway.

One Saturday, Tobias and I were sitting in the visiting room. He was eating a cheeseburger. I said "Tobias, around the last of October or the first of November, you're going to be a daddy, again." He stopped eating and his eyes set directly on mine. He never said one thing but I could tell he was overjoyed. In man's eyes, this child was never meant to be but God said "be" and that was that. As Tobias regained some composure, I remember us walking around the visiting room, him telling some of his friends, "It's in there", while patting my stomach."

Chapter 27

The children were very excited about momma having another baby, especially little John Lee. When I told dad, he said, "Cheryl, you were pregnant before you even got married, that is why you did it." I didn't even respond to him. I told mom that I was having a baby but, in her state of mind, I don't think she ever believed me. She would always say in her little voice that was not so understandable at times, "No you're not, no you're not." As I begin to show, the officers and other staff members at the prison surely believed it. I found myself facing new hostilities now to go along with the old ones. I was called "a whore, a slut," and probably a lot more names that I don't even know about, but it really didn't matter to me. I had been called worse in my life. I personally felt there should have been conjugal visitation for husbands and wives anyway. A few of the officers were very nice and gave me their blessings while others were very open and unashamed in asking me about my personal business. They would ask, "How in the world did you get pregnant," or "Is it the inmates baby?" I thought them not only bold but stupid as well but I would simply answer their question of how in the world I got pregnant by simply responding, "It was done through a process called sexual reproduction. I assure you it was not by Immaculate Conception." This would really piss them off.

As weeks went by, I learned that I again had placenta previa. As with Michael, hearing that I had placenta previa was scary but not as scary as now. I didn't have any medical knowledge or hands on experience in providing nursing care to women with placenta previa or any other complication related to pregnancy when I was pregnant with Michael. Now, with this baby, I had acquired a lot more medical knowledge and had seen a lot more. I was very upset when the doctor told me this because I wanted this baby with all my heart and I knew how much Tobias wanted this baby too. Tobias called me at home to check to see how my doctor's appointment went. When I told him about the previa, he immediately began to soothe me. He said, "Sweetheart, don't worry about anything. If it's God's will, this baby will be born and everything will be alright. If not, it will still be God's will." Even though his words of comfort did not comfort me much, I appreciated his view on things.

Working only on weekends was a blessing indeed at this particular point in my life. I was instructed by the doctor to just lie down most of the time and get plenty of rest. He said hopefully resting would resolve the previa. Being home all week afforded me all the rest I needed. I felt really bad most of the time anyway, really tired, so I really didn't feel like doing much else but lying down. Cherylyn and I would attend to mom's needs as usual, and I would muster up enough energy to attend Tee-ball and softball games and school activities, but it seemed like everything I did was an effort. Nevertheless, I sailed on through like a champ. I'm glad no one could tell how

I really felt; at least, I hope no one could. At work, the girls in OB were very nice and went out of their way to make me comfortable as well. Dr. Crowe was my obstetrician. I worked alongside him in so many deliveries, vaginal as well as cesarean sections. He was a very good doctor but his bedside manners sometimes left a lot to be desired. He was an ex-military doctor and I attributed his mannerisms to that for the most part. I felt reassured that, if I did have any complications with the placenta previa, I would be right there in OB where I could be placed on a monitor and have the doctor easily accessible. That was my main reason for choosing Dr. Crowe. I didn't want to be far away from my children when I delivered or if I should have further complications and have to be hospitalized.

I made my weekend trips to see Tobias and for the most part, I was beginning to feel better. I remember being very moody sometimes, not in a mean kind of way, but in a tearful kind of way. This would blow Tobias' mind totally. He had never been in such close proximity with a pregnant woman before so he didn't have a clue as what to expect from me. I remember on one occasion, I must have irritated him to his wits end that day. I don't even remember what I did now. I do remember him telling me to go home and get some rest. This was the one and only time I can ever remember him ending our visit, not the officers calling for the end of visitation when it was over. On most occasions though, the children, Tobias, and I would have really good visits. He would sit there and play and wrestle with the children, play games with them, eat chicken and cheeseburgers with them and rub my stomach. He loved to feel the baby moving around and kicking. Tobias tried to teach me how to play some of the games he had taught the children but I must have had a brain freeze for the totality of my pregnancy. I just could not get the hang of most of the games. This would cause him to loose some patience with me but he remained very loving anyway.

In my third trimester, I begin to have problems with my blood pressure going up. I was given orders by the doctor to remain calm for the remainder of my pregnancy. That was kind of hard with all of the things I had to do in a day's time. Even though I was married, I still had to be mom and dad for the children, I had to help take care of mom and I had to work, but I did my best to comply. Dr. Crowe also gave me a prescription for blood pressure medicine, something I had never given thought as to me having to take them. Dr. Crowe also did an ultrasound. On ultrasound, Dr. Crowe said, "It's a girl." He also said that the previa was completely resolved now but he was concerned about my blood pressure. For this reason he said, if I didn't go into labor on my own, he wanted to induce my labor. So I rested, watched what I ate, the whole nine yards, but my blood pressure remained higher than normal.

About three weeks before my due date, Dr. Crowe called me into his office. He said he wanted to try inducing my labor. I was all for it. I was very heavy with baby and I was tired of walking around looking like the Goodyear blimp. When I saw the children off to school this particular morning, I took my little overnight bag and went to the hospital. Once there, an IV was started on me and I was given something called Pitocin. This medicine was supposed to start my contractions regularly. Well, I lay there all day long and nothing happened. When it was time for the children to come home, I asked Dr. Crowe if he would please release me to go home to see about my children. He did. When I arrived home, the children were disappointed that I had not had the baby, especially little John Lee. They were glad to see me anyway though. That weekend, I told Tobias about that experience of having to get stuck to start an IV, then lying there all day long without the first contraction, not even a Braxton-Hicks contraction. He just sat there listening to me patiently and rubbing my stomach. When the baby started kicking around, Tobias would start talking to the baby. To be such a rough neck, Tobias surely was as gentle as a lamb when it came to me and the children, even the unborn one. I told Tobias that Dr. Crowe wanted me to come back to the hospital on Monday morning after leaving work and getting the children off to school. I also told him that I wasn't too thrilled about it and was pondering whether to go or not. Tobias continued to soothe our little kicking machine as he told me, "Sweetheart, go on back like the doctor wants you to. I'm concerned about this high blood pressure and I don't want to loose you." Well, he talked me into going back for more Pitocin.

True to my word, I came back to the hospital after getting my babies off to school. I again went through the ritual and pain of having an IV started. As many as I had started on other people, I had this personal thing about needles, I hated them when they were aimed at my veins. Anyway, I lay there all day long with the Pitocin dripping at the maximum safest rate possible, and still, no contractions. I could not eat anything and the ice chips thing had gotten very old indeed. I was "fit to be tied" as mom would have said. I was too through with all of this stuff. I'd had four babies beforehand, had them all naturally and I had never had to go through any of these formalities. I was resigning myself to the fact that I would certainly be pregnant forever!! I left the hospital that evening feeling very down trodden and disappointed. When I arrived home to meet and greet my little tribe, they were very happy to see me, pregnant and all. Just seeing how much they were happy to see me and listening to their day's activities made me forget about my disappointment, for a while anyway.

It was the weekend again and I went to the prison, very down trodden in my spirits. When Tobias came into the visiting room, my spirits were no higher. I told him that I had lain there in that hospital bed, again, all day long with not the first contraction. Despite taking the blood pressure medicine just as it was ordered, my blood pressure remained high. I told him I was going to the doctor every week now and I was tired of the whole thing. He just sat there quietly listening to me vent. I told him that Dr. Crowe wanted me to come back to try induction again on Monday morning but that I wasn't going. Then Tobias said, "Sweetheart, now listen, you are not going to be pregnant forever so just stop saying that. I know you're tired and miserable but I want you to go back to the hospital on Monday morning and do exactly what the doctor wants you to, okay?" Well, I really wasn't okay with any of it, but after much coaxing from Tobias I gave him my word that I would go back on Monday morning. I was beginning to feel as though I lived at the hospital.

So, Monday morning came and I again, saw the children off to school. I had gotten in the habit of leaving the overnight bag packed and right there by my bedroom door. After getting all cleaned up, I picked up the bag and headed out of the house to "my second home." Once there, an IV was again started and I just lay there all day long. My dad had come by to see me after his morning routine, getting mom's breakfast and needs all taken care of, then coming up to the hospital to have his breakfast and to get his socialization in. As much as he was against this marriage and pregnancy, when he came to the room where I was, he tried to console me. I appreciated that. It was about 12:45 pm and still, no contractions. My blood pressure was slowly creeping up as the Pitocin drip was almost at the highest rate it could safely be. Dr. Crowe came over to the hospital from his office which was right across the street. He checked my cervix and I had not dilated at all. Then, about an hour later, something miraculous happened; I began to have contractions. I had forgotten how much they hurt, till now that is. I wanted Tobias here with me more than ever. I called dad and asked him if he would please go and pick up Cherylyn from school and bring her to the hospital with me. He said that he would do it as soon as he finished feeding mom lunch. I was relieved to hear that. It was about 2:00 pm now and I was hurting really badly and still, no Cherylyn. My blood pressure was getting dangerously high and Dr. Crowe came in and ordered the nurses to start Magnesium Sulfate on me as well. This medicine was supposed to help my blood pressure to go back down. The nurses also inserted a foley catheter in my bladder and boy was that uncomfortable for me. I knew then that I would have a new appreciation for my patients that I had to insert an IV and a foley catheter in from that moment on. Despite all of these interventions, my blood pressure continued to rise. Cherylyn arrived at the hospital around 2:30 pm and I was having full blown contractions now. I called out to her and asked that she come in and let me hold her hand. She came inside and put her hand in mine, but when I had a contraction, she snatched her hand away. She said, "Momma, you're hurting my hand." I suppose I was but I didn't mean to. Cherylyn stayed outside of my room and peeked her head in the door every now and then. It was now 3:00 and my blood pressure continued to rise. Dr. Crowe had the nurses prepare me for a cesarean section. I had never had any kind of surgery before, but at that moment, it didn't matter what they did to me. I just wanted this excruciating pain to stop! Just as the nurses were preparing to carry me around to the operating room, my water broke. It was green colored or medically known as meconium stained, which indicated that the baby was in some sort of distress and had a bowel movement inside of me prior to delivery. When Dr. Crowe checked my cervix, I was fully dilated and I had the strongest urge to push. The bed was broken down and my feet were placed in stirrups. Dr. Crowe pulled my hips to the bottom of the bed and in his usual, military voice screamed at me to "Push." Then the other nurses chimed in, "Push." Everyone was telling me something and I was confused for a minute. As it turned out, I wasn't pushing for very long when I received the command from Dr. Crowe to "Stop pushing and just breathe." The baby's head was out and all that could be seen was a head filled with the prettiest, straightest, blackest hair that I had ever seen. Dr. Crowe said at that point, "Yes, it's a girl with a head full of hair." The umbilical cord was wrapped around the baby's neck so Dr. Crowe asked that I stopped pushing so he could get the cord from around the neck. As hard as it was, I just lay there panting. Then before I knew it, the rest of the baby seemingly flew right out of me. Well, to my surprise, and I believe everyone else's, my newborn baby girl had a penis. It was a boy, a beautiful boy, perfectly normal and healthy. Cherylyn came inside the room when she heard the baby cry. I just lay there shaking uncontrollably as if it were 10 below in the room and looking at the baby and Cherylyn. After bonding briefly with the baby, he was taken to the newborn nursery and I just lay there saying, "Thank you God," over and over again.

Chapter 28

The children were very excited when they learned they had a new baby brother. Even though Boobie only had a learner's permit, I allowed him to drive the car back home from the hospital where I parked it that morning. The children wanted to see the baby and I didn't feel comfortable with them walking to the hospital. I didn't want to keep asking dad for favors either. Besides, Boobie was an excellent driver; he just didn't have his license yet. John Lee especially bonded with the baby. He just sat there on my hospital bed and stared and stared and stared at the baby until it was time for them to leave. Michael was pleased with the baby as well but he didn't moon over him like John Lee did. Tyrone Jr., who had a very quiet disposition anyway, just sat on my bed smiling as he watched everyone else interact with the baby. I teased Cherylyn about not being able to stay in the room with me and help me through labor. She said, "Momma, you were hurting my hand real bad." I'm sure I did squeeze her hand too hard, but I believe she was more afraid than anything else. I'm sure she was able to see my tonsils with every contraction. That would probably have scared anybody. After a lengthy visit and supper at the hospital, Boobie loaded everyone up in our family car and took them home so he and Cherylyn could prepare everyone for school the next day. I assured them I would be home at least by Wednesday if not before. After the children arrived home, I called to make sure they were alright. As I was talking to them, Tobias beeped in. Boobie connected us on three-way. Tobias was overjoyed to learn that I had the baby and both of us were doing fine. I told him, "There's one catch Sweetheart, he's a boy, not a girl. How do you feel about that?" His reply was "Sweetheart, every man wants a son." Months before, Tobias and I discussed names and thankfully, we picked out one for a boy and a girl. I wanted to name the baby after Tobias but he wouldn't hear of it. He said he never liked his middle name and for that reason, he did not want to give it to his son. So we named the baby Malcolm. Tobias was as pleased as punch; I could hear it in his voice.

The next morning, another one of the doctors that I worked with came to see me. Her name was Dr. K. or so I nicknamed her. She was concerned about my blood pressure. It still had not come down. I had never before in my life had any problems with high blood pressure, although mom and dad were hypertensive. Dr. K told me that it just might be gestational and if that were the case, it should and would begin to gradually go back down. I felt more relieved after hearing her say that. After breakfast and a shower, I was feeling better than I had in months. I called the nursery and asked them to bring Malcolm to me. He was such a beautiful baby. He was a good-natured baby and he only cried when he was hungry or needed a diaper change. God had indeed given us another little miracle, a little piece of heaven on earth.

Though dad had not been happy about my marriage or

my pregnancy, after eating breakfast and making his daily chaplain rounds, he would come to my room and sit there talking to me. He would say, "Cheryl that sure is a fine baby. He's as fine a baby as I've ever seen. I know your mama wants to see him." I anticipated having a one night stay, perhaps two at the most but as it turned out, I stayed the entire week. I was too through. My blood pressure refused to return to normal readings and I was still very swollen. I wanted to be at home with the other children and I became very upset about this, which of course, did not help my blood pressure problems at all. Dad came in every morning and seeing that I was very upset about my present situation, would try to console me. He assured me that the children were okay because he "checked on them" and they were going to school and getting there on time. He said Boobie and Cherylyn were handling things like little adults. This news still didn't make me feel any better but I just sat there in bed smiling back at him as tears rolled down my cheeks.

It was now Thursday and this was my 3rd day after delivery. Dr. K still wanted me to stay another day because she was not pleased with my blood pressure. I reasoned with her that it was obvious I was just going to have to continue taking blood pressure medicine. I asked her to write me a script and let me go home. She started me on another medicine but she said she wanted to keep me "today" just to see how the medicine worked. Her news was not what I wanted to hear but I didn't want to be non-compliant, so I reluctantly stayed for another day. Tobias was beside himself with worry. He had his counselor calling, an officer, whomever would be kind enough to allow him to call me. He asked, "Sweetheart, what's wrong with you, is the baby okay, when are you coming home, are you going to be able to visit with the baby this weekend?"

The questions went on and on and on. I assured him that Malcolm was just great and that I was getting there. He reluctantly hung up when the time allotted for him to talk to me was up.

Chapter 29

At last, Friday morning came and I was so ready to go home. Dr. Crowe gave me my discharge clearance. Boobie had driven the car back to the hospital the previous evening and Dad carried the children back home for me. I told the children on Thursday evening that "Momma will be coming home tomorrow." As usual Dad came to my room after eating breakfast and visiting. He kept asking me "Are you sure you're coming over to see your mama, I know she really wants to see the baby." I know dad kept asking me if I were going to come over for sure because lately I would tell him I was coming over to their house, only not to show up. I know this was wrong, not to mention undependable on my part, but I was tired of going over to visit them because dad mostly just fussed about one thing or another. He never seemed to appreciate anything that was done for him. I talked to Tobias about this at one point. I said, "Tobias, I really miss mom and I love to go over and spend time with her but I do get so tired of being around dad." Tobias would listen attentively and then tell me, "Sweetheart, go on over to visit your mom and dad. You know that mom needs you so just ignore dad." I thought this was very sweet and thoughtful coming from a man that dad had chosen not to even like, much less attempt to get to know. I listened to Tobias' advice for the most part. Anyway, I assured dad that I would certainly come over to see mom before going on home.

With my discharge paperwork in my bag and my baby in my arms, I was wheeled out to the parking lot. The student nurse that wheeled me outside seemed very shocked that I didn't have anyone waiting to carry me home. After securing the car seat for Malcolm and putting him in it, the nurse asked, "Are you going to drive yourself home?" I replied, "Yes I am dear." If this little nurse only knew how much of a pro I had become when it came to doing things for myself by myself. I told her how much I appreciated her concern and her care that morning and I drove off heading straight for mom's house. When I went inside mom's house, dad had gotten her up for the morning and she was sitting at the dining room window in her wheelchair. She was glad to see me when I came into the dining room and she started smiling. The stroke had twisted her face somewhat and her right side was mostly flaccid, so I put Malcolm in her left arm. Mom was left handed anyway so I suppose having her right side affected was somewhat of a blessing in disguise. As soon as I placed Malcolm in her arm, she bent her face down to his and just sat there kissing him and looking at him. Every now and then mom would look at me and ask "Whose baby is this?" I would continue to say, "Mom, it's my baby." She would always reply, "No it's not" but she loved him anyway. After spending a couple hours with mom, I kissed her and dad and left for my little trailer of a home. Even though the trailer needed every kind of repair from A to Z, I was still very happy to be going home. Once

home, I placed Malcolm in his crib, the same crib that Michael
had slept in. After much repairing on this crib, John Lee had
been able to use it as well. Now, this same little crib that was
originally Orlando's crib, had withstood Michael's rail tearing to accommodate John Lee and now Malcolm. I had not
done very much of anything yet I felt tired. Malcolm continued to be a very good little baby and he went to sleep for the
remainder of the morning and into early evening. I lay down
and was able to take a nap before the phone started ringing.
It was Tobias. He was overjoyed that I had finally come home.
He wanted to make sure I was okay and that I would feel up
to visiting him in the morning. I assured him that I was feeling better and we would come to see him for sure. Tobias was
overjoyed and excited about seeing his son for the first time.
Before he hung up, I could hear the jubilance in his voice. That
made me happy as well. What I hadn't mentioned was that
instead of being able to go back to work in two weeks as I had
originally planned; because of my blood pressure Dr. Crowe
was not going to let me come back until another month. When
he told me that, I initially started to worry about how in the
world we were going to make it. Then I stopped and looked
back on all the times in my life, our lives, where God provided
for us and brought us through our trials and I relaxed.

The children came home on schedule. They were all glad
to have me back home. After my nap and talking with Tobias,
I had gotten up and prepared a very nice dinner for my little ones. John Lee just wanted to sit and look at Malcolm; he
wasn't very excited about dinner. He loved his baby brother.
He had drawn a picture in school of him and his baby brother that day. He told me he drew it for Malcolm. There were
two little stick people on the paper, the longer figure being
John Lee. After insisting that John Lee eat his dinner, I let him

hold Malcolm. That really made his evening. I was so glad to be home with all of my babies. I missed them so much. After hearing about everything that had gone on in school that day with them all, I was beginning to get very tired. I made sure the children were all comfortable and then I settled down to prepare for bed. Surprisingly, Malcolm only woke up for a feeding and a diaper change and he'd go right back to sleep afterward. I really appreciated that, especially this night.

The next morning, I decided to take Cherylyn with me to visit Tobias so she could help me with Malcolm. Once we reached the prison, there were so many inquisitive officers, or so it seemed to me. Many of them were asking to see the baby. I wonder if some of them wanted to see just how an inmate's baby looked. No matter what their reasons, when I allowed them to woo over Malcolm, all of their conclusions were the same. Malcolm was a very good looking baby. One of the officers said, "He looks Hispanic." I guess she thought so because of Malcolm's fair complexion and straight, black hair, I don't know. After much going on about how "sweet and pretty" Malcolm was, we finally reached the visiting room. As soon as I approached the door, I saw Tobias pacing back and forth in the visiting room. When the door was opened, Tobias immediately came to the door and took Malcolm from Cherylyn's arms. He led the way to the table and helped me to get comfortable in my seat. After kissing me and Cherylyn, he took Malcolm's blanket off and he examined him from head to toe, literally. When Tobias pulled Malcolm's diaper off to change him, Malcolm peed right in his face. Tobias just laughed and said, "Sweetheart, did you see that?" Indeed I had and I laughed and laughed too. After the diaper change, Tobias fed Malcolm. When burping Malcolm, he spit up a lot of formula on Tobias' shirt. Tobias was really getting it from both ends this day and he seemed to be enjoying every minute of it. After a short time, Tobias just got up from the table and holding Malcolm in a football hold that he'd read about during my pregnancy, just strutted around the visiting room with his son, strutting as proud as any peacock ever could have, stopping at different tables to show off Malcolm. I don't think I've ever seen Tobias quite that happy and proud as he was this day. Tobias was never one to verbalize his immediate, most intimate feelings right away. Instead, it was a few days after his first seeing Malcolm when I received the most beautiful, handmade card from Tobias. It was a card to thank me for having his son, so perfect and beautiful. It read:

A Message To My Wife

Thank you for our son. Sweetheart, thank you for having our son; two eyes, ten fingers, ten toes, and a perfect little nose. I will love and cherish him as well as you. He will need these things while his life is still new… With all my love! Tobias

I'd had four babies previously and this was the very first time I had ever received anything but, as mom would say, "A hard way to go and a short time to get there," for having a baby for him. I was very humbled by Tobias' thoughtfulness and thankfulness.

Chapter 30

Malcolm grew quickly it seemed. He was a very inquisitive baby and he noticed everything. I don't think anything got past him. He was such a loved baby. His sister and brothers were all crazy about him. He loved them as well. When I worked on weekends, Boobie and Cherylyn babysat him. Cherylyn later told me that Boobie always chose to keep Malcolm on Saturday nights so he wouldn't have to wake up to feed him on Sunday night, the night before school. I'm just so thankful that they both really didn't mind keeping the children because they knew I had to work to take care of us. Tobias was ecstatic to spend time with all the children every weekend. He divided his time up with each child so that no one would feel left out. He enjoyed feeding Malcolm some of his cheeseburgers or chicken and Malcolm enjoyed it too. Tobias would chew the food and put it in Malcolm's little mouth and the both of them would sit there smacking. I enjoyed watching Tobias interact with the children. He was really very good with them. Another thing I loved about Tobias was that he never, ever forgot one of the children's birthdays or special occasions. He would always send them a card, even if he had to make it himself or have it made by another inmate. He always wanted to keep abreast of every aspect of their lives as well. He always offered good, sound advice wherever and whenever needed. I would kid him sometimes and ask him "Sweetheart, are you sure you've never been a parent before? You don't have a house full of children somewhere do you?" He'd just smile.

When Malcolm was a few months old, Cherylyn read to him often. When he was almost a year old, she would draw dots that spelled his name and she taught him how to trace the dots to spell his name. She was really good with him. John Lee loved hanging out with his little brother too. It was as if the two of them were joined at the hip. Michael loved to mess around with Malcolm too but most of the time, Michael was hanging out in the trailer court with another little guy that lived in the trailer court as well. His name was Devonte and he was just as busy and mischievous as Michael was. Tyrone Jr. was working at a restaurant, so that, and school occupied most of his time. All in all, everything was going well. I was still focused on buying a house for the children. We were blessed to have a roof over our heads but that is just about all that we had left of the trailer, the roof. We had to have a more secure home. Even with everything that we needed and didn't have, just having Tobias to love and to return love to me and the children propelled me on through and motivated me to keep moving forward. I was able to smile in the midst of my trials and tribulations. I once heard a preacher say, "You have to think yourself happy." After pondering that thought, I decided that this was what I would do, regardless. So, from that day on, I tried to keep a smile on my face. No matter how frustrated, sad, worried, whatever, I would "think myself happy."

Cherylyn was in the eighth grade; Boobie the tenth. One day Cherylyn came home from school and said, "Momma, we have a brother and his name is Terry." Well, you can imagine that I was totally floored. I went on to ask her about this Terry person. She told me that he was in the same grade as she was and he was really nice. I told her to invite Terry over to the house on the upcoming weekend. Surely enough, Terry came to visit us. When I saw him initially, he looked just like Boobie and Michael. Boobie and Michael have always looked just like Tyrone so I began asking questions. I learned that Terry's birthday was in September, just two months after Cherylyn's, and in the very same year. I had heard something about Tyrone having a child a long time ago and when I asked him about it, of course, he denied it on Martha's life. Now, all I knew was this child was here and I would love him just like my very own. I realized that Terry, like my children, was just as much a victim. He was brought into this world yet never knew the love of a real father. Thus, a long friendship started. Terry came over often to visit us and was even able to spend the nights with us on some weekends. Once I found out what his favorite foods were, I would fix them for him. I've always loved to cook for people because I enjoyed seeing them enjoy my cooking. I've always gotten a real kick out of making other people happy. Terry was no different. I was so thankful that my children had been given the opportunity to get to know Terry and to love him and he them. I harbored no ill-feelings toward Terry's mother either. What would have been the rationale for it anyway?

Chapter 31

Mom stopped eating like she should. It seemed that it was difficult for her to swallow her foods and she would take it out of her mouth and put it in her plate. She had no problem swallowing a piece of cake or something sweet and I never quite made the connection with that. Anyway, she was loosing weight as well. Dad would have to call the ambulance for her more often and she was now being admitted to the hospital more often as well. Whenever she was in the hospital, Dad would come up for breakfast and spend the entire day with her. I would come in the morning and give her a bath and make sure she was comfortable. On weekends, because I was already at work, I could check on her often. I also continued to do her bowel treatments when she was in the hospital. When she came home the last time from the hospital, John Lee, Jr. hired another lady to help take care of mom. Martha had long since stopped coming to help them. This little lady, Ms. Carr, was just that, a very short, little lady with grey eyes. When I came over to see how things were going with Ms. Carr and mom, mom said, "She's mean," plain as day. I was very observant of her from that moment on. As it turned out, not only was she mean, she was nasty as well. I would sit there in the kitchen talking with her as she prepared supper. She would take any kind of meat from the freezer to prepare together, like, ground beef and chicken. I had never seen that done ever before. Then, she would make biscuits. I would watch her and almost heave as she would be mixing the dough for the biscuits when she would stop, pick her nose, roll her fingers together and pluck something from them, then start to mix the biscuits again, all in one breath. I was sick to my stomach for a while after that. John Lee and Michael would always want some of her bread after my forbidding them to eat anything! I could have rung their necks. I also noticed that when she repositioned mom, she talked sharply to her and pulled on her too hard. I spoke to her then and asked that she please be gentler with mom. I had been taught to respect my elders but this little old lady was about to get knocked out. I told dad about it and needless to say, Ms. Carr's employment longevity was not long at all.

Mom still was not eating well. The doctor wanted to insert a feeding tube in her stomach and that was a difficult decision for dad to make. After he talked with each of us, he decided to let the doctor go ahead with it. Evelyn was very opposed to the surgery. She felt that if "we took our time to feed mom, she would eat." Well, we were taking our time to feed mom, I know for sure, dad took his time to feed her and to take care of her period. Mom just would not eat. So, the ambulance came to get her on the morning of surgery. When I arrived at mom's hospital room, there she was, sitting up in bed looking from dad to me but not saying anything. That morning, mom looked better to me than she had looked in years. Her skin was glowing and she just lay there with the most calm look and prettiest smile I had seen in a long time. The surgery was scheduled around 12:00 noon. I went to get lunch for dad and me and brought it back to the room. I know mom was hungry because she had not eaten anything since the evening before. It was kind of thoughtless of me to be sitting here eating in front of her, knowing she couldn't eat anything, but I didn't want to leave her side any longer than I had to either. Mom kept looking from my plate to dad's plate and smiling. Shortly after we finished lunch, the nurses took mom away to the operating room. I left to go home and put Malcolm down for his nap. After the surgery, I would come back to check on mom.

When I arrived in mom's hospital room, there she was, lying there in that bed, heaving and heaving and having all kinds of respiratory distress. Dad was just sitting there by her bed holding her hand. For the first time in my life, dad looked very defeated. I don't know what emotions I was having. I panicked when I saw mom like this. All I could think about was when I left her, she looked great. This was a complete turnaround. She was on continuous monitoring and her blood pressure readings were very high. Then I noticed that her intravenous fluid was normal saline. I was rattling off millions of questions all in one breath, or so it seemed. I was asking the nurse that was at her bedside, "What did you do to my mother, why is she struggling to breathe, why do you have salt water going through her veins if her blood pressure is so high?" The nurse just looked at me. Dad must have seen how my behavior was quickly escalating so he sent me around to the admissions office with mom's Medicare card. I can't say now how I reached the office because I don't remember walking there. I do know that as I was standing in line for service, Vee walked past on her way to work. I hollered out to her and ran to her at the same time. When I reached her, Vee said, "Girl, how are you doing?" I couldn't answer her question. I just broke down right there in the middle of the hallway. I was crying uncontrollably. Vee, with her sweet, compassionate self, just hugged me and led me to the OB dept. and into our little break room. She let me cry on her shoulder until I couldn't cry any more tears. Then she talked to me about how God picks his favorite flowers and how mom had suffered so long and she needed rest if that was God's will. After her talking to me, I felt some better. It seemed that Vee had always been there for me when I really needed someone and this time was no different. I will always hold Vee in high esteem for her genuine friendship down through the years.

A week passed and mom was no better. She was comatose for the most part and when I came into the room, she didn't even know me. This hurt more than I can find the words to describe. The doctor called for all of the children to come to see her and I knew this was not good news. So, my sisters and brothers all came from all over to see mom. I was at work and it was so busy in OB that evening, I couldn't even break away to join them. Later, after things slowed down somewhat, I went to mom's room but everyone had left, everyone but dad. I asked dad, "Did mom recognize anyone?" He replied, "Yes, she called them all by name." Well, this really did hurt me. I kept thinking, "I'm the one who has been here with her all of this time and she doesn't even know who I am." I went to her bedside and rubbed her hair and her face and she never opened her eyes. She just lay there and grunted often as if she were in pain. This was so unnerving for me. I could not stand to see her so sick, yet not be able to communicate her pain, her needs. I kissed her and talked with dad. He was very tired and he looked it. I told him to go on home and get some rest and to come in the morning to see mom. He hated to leave her side but finally he went home. I stayed a while longer and then I went back to my department. I went to the lounge and I cried as I prayed, "God, please don't let her suffer any more. She's suffered for so long and she's been such a good person and a great wife and mother. Please God; take her out of her suffering." After composing myself somewhat, I returned to the floor to check on my patients. About 2:00 am, the charge nurse whose name was Kim came to the desk where I was sitting charting on my patient and she says, "Cheryl, come with me." I said, "Why, what's wrong?" She said, "It's your mother, she passed away." "What do you mean, passed away" I asked? I was horror stricken. I stood but my legs went limp so Kim pulled a wheelchair from the corner and helped me to sit down in it. I was screaming by now. All I could say was "Lord Jesus, Lord Jesus." Kim pushed me through the hallways to mom's room and I'm sure I made quite a scene on the ride there. I certainly didn't mean to but I couldn't stop crying and saying Lord Jesus. Once in mom's room, Kim left me alone to be with her. She looked so peaceful lying there. She looked like she was in a deep, pleasant sleep, nothing like what I had seen of her only hours before. I talked to her and told her that I had prayed for God to take her with Him so she wouldn't have to suffer anymore. I told her that I felt so guilty because I had prayed that God take her from us. I told her that I loved her so very much and that she had been the best mother any child could have been blessed with. After sitting there at mom's bedside for what seemed like hours, I finally composed myself and went back to OB. I was excused from the rest of my shift so I left to go to dad's house. I awakened him from a very deep sleep and told him the news. He just sat there on the side of the bed looking at nothing really. Then he said, "I started to spend the night with Honey, I sure wish I had." I said, "Dad, let's just go to the hospital so you can see her." He dressed and we went back to the hospital. Once in mom's room, I left him so that he could have some time alone with mom. I felt like a zombie, but I knew I had to pull it together because I had to tell the children and my sisters and brothers as well. When I arrived home, I woke the children and told them that Grandma had gone to heaven to be with the Lord. Cherylyn took the news very badly and she began to cry so pitifully. She was very close to her grandmother and she loved her so much. John Lee and Michael were crying too. Boobie just stood there trying to comfort the rest of us. I woke Malcolm and loaded all the children in the car and we went back to the hospital so that everyone could say their last goodbyes.

Chapter 32

This was a totally new experience for me, for all of us. I had gone to lots of funerals before but I had never loss any one of my immediate loved ones. I basically just went through the days like I was programmed or something. I just felt so empty, yet full of sadness. I really can't find the words to precisely describe how I was feeling. Going to the funeral home with dad and my brothers and sisters was an odd, eerie feeling. It felt really weird walking around in the back shopping for coffins. I'm glad I had my family there with me though because I found strength in them through this ordeal. We had all lost someone very precious to us, the very core of the family, the glue that had, for years brought and held the family together. Evelyn, Doll and I wanted mom to have on something very befitting of her. We each, at the same time, saw this white gown hanging up. It was made of silk and lace and it had a pearl collar. It was very dainty and beautiful, just like mom was. There was no question about it, we wanted mom to have this gown. It's so funny that my sisters and I can be miles and miles apart, yet, when we come together, we find that we've bought items that are very similar, if not the same. We each love each other's styles. This day was no different. After all the arrangements were completed, dad went back home with Aunt Rae and my brothers, my sisters and I went to eat lunch. We tried to go on and act as normal as we could but we each knew that mamma would never be with us again in this life.

At last, we all had to come together at the funeral home again. We had to look at mom and make sure everything was okay before the public viewing. When I saw mom, she was the most beautiful I had seen her since her long seven year illness. She looked so peaceful laying there. Her hair was done just beautifully and the gown that we picked out was just the perfect one for her. I just stood there and stared and stared for the longest time. We were well pleased with how mom looked, the coffin, everything was beautiful. The employees placed mom in the front window of the funeral parlor so that everyone who passed by could see her. I used to ride by frequently just to stare at her.

To this day, I cannot understand why it is that the grieving family has to entertain guests all day long and half the night. I'm sure people meant well but boy was it tiring. I really didn't feel much like talking a lot but dad's house was never empty. People would bring over foods, drinks, anything they thought might be needed and I really did appreciate everyone's acts of love and kindness. Then there was the wake. Mom's family and friends came to the chapel and everyone sat there talking and socializing. I was sitting beside my cousin Bonnie, Aunt Rae's daughter. She was so pitiful. She didn't say a word but she just cried and cried. All of Aunt Rae's children were there because they loved "Sister" as they affectionately nicknamed mom. After a while, people took turns saying nice and true things about mom. After about two hours, this was over and

I was glad. The next day was the funeral and I was glad to be bringing some closure to this. I sat on the front row right beside dad at the church. John Lee, Jr. was sitting right behind me and he kept tapping me and asking if I were okay. I was doing my best to hold things together and I did for the most part. Aunt Rae and her children sang a very nice song for mom as her son played the organ. A lot of the nurses from my department were there and I thought that was very sweet of them. I really don't remember much else that went on. I do remember that when it was the family's turn to view mom for the last time, when dad stood up, it was as if his knees were made of jello and the other preachers had to grab him or he certainly would have fallen to the floor. It tore my heart apart when I saw that and I cried for dad more than for me at that moment. Soon we were on our way outside. I had done very well holding it together inside the church but when we were outside and I saw Evelyn and Doll, I came up to them. I remember crying while telling them, "Y'all, momma's gone, momma's gone." We just stood there, us hugging each other. My mother-n-law was with me during this great loss in my life and I thank and love her so much for thinking enough of me and my family to travel to be with us at this difficult time in our lives.

Well, it was finally over. I watched until the very end. After the men lowered mom's casket into the ground, we got back in our cars. We went back to the church where there was more food and more socializing. I really didn't feel much like it but I made it through anyway. When we all returned to dad's house, the family was sitting around making plans to get together for more than just a sad event. Dad started right in with opposition to the idea. He then began passing blame as to why mom died. He said things like "Orlando worried honey to death and Cheryl didn't make it any better, running away from home and worrying her half to death. Then she brought Honey some Easter eggs home knowing full well she didn't need them." Evelyn sat there and listened until she'd had enough. Finally she said, "Dad, you did your part of worrying mama in case you don't realize it. You fussed from sun up to sun down and she could never do anything to please you." Dad was silent then and never said another word. I just sat there in the living room with all of the numerous family members, yet I felt so all alone. I remember wishing with all my heart that Tobias could have been with me. I needed his physical presence, his strength, his soothing now more than ever. The next day I went to visit Tobias because I needed a Tobias fix more than ever. It was so, so good to see him, to be held by him if only for a short while. I had brought one of the programs from mom's funeral with me but I wasn't sure whether I'd be allowed to carry it in or not. Thankfully, one officer had compassion for me and allowed me to carry it in so Tobias could see it. We sat there at the table quietly for the most part but I could feel Tobias' undivided attention. He had this way of generating comforting, soothing emotions deep within me without even saying one word.

Dad observed me and saw how happy I would be whenever I spoke with or visited Tobias. Once he told me "Cheryl, I really believe Tobias loves you." That was the closest dad ever came to giving me his blessings.

Dad was very lonely after mom's death. I tried to spend as much time with him as I could. He didn't fuss like he used to and that made being around him much more pleasant. I could only imagine what it would feel like to lose someone that you've been around for the last 56 years of your life. What a lonesome feeling that has to be. Looking back I cannot recall a night that dad wasn't at home and if he wasn't home, mom

knew just where he was. He would be only a telephone call
away. He continued to go to the hospital every morning to
have his breakfast and to visit people that were sick. He continued to preach and travel to different churches to preach but
he would always say how much he missed "Honey." Dad was
basically a very healthy man. He had worked hard all of his
life. He stayed busy doing something or another. He didn't like
to see people just hanging around doing nothing. He would
often say, "You'll never get anywhere in life just sitting around
on your stool of do nothing." He lived by his words. It was always his wish to "Live to be three score and ten" and "To just
preach my sermon and when I'm finished, just die right there
in the pulpit."

It was the late fall of the year. My car was not working so
once again we had no transportation. As I was thinking back
on our lives so far, my children and I had been very accustomed to doing without things that we needed and this time
was no different. I came to the realization that during the most
trying times in my life, God had always worked everything out
for me, for us, one way or another and this time would be no
different. I believe the purpose of trials and tribulations are to
know that we really can't do anything on our own or for ourselves but that we must ask God to help us and lean on Him
and believe that He will do just that. I believe that troubles in
our lives only make us stronger, more humble and more faithful, I know mine have. I was determined that my main focus
was to have a nice home for my children; a car had to be put
on the back burner for now. So, in the middle of the winter, I
again, stepped right out there on faith, with the biggest smile
on my face that one could imagine. I didn't have any money
for a house, but I contacted a realtor anyway. We, the realtor,
my little man Boobie, and I rode around looking for houses.

We finally found two that were just perfect for us. After much indecision, I finally chose the ranch. It was just lovely. It was in a very convenient part of town, one that I knew I could walk back and forth to work without any problem. The neighborhood was nice too. The yard was huge and it had lots and lots of beautiful trees and flowers; almost as pretty as mom had kept her yard. There were three bedrooms so finally Cherylyn would have her own bedroom. There was only one bathroom but that didn't dampen my spirits or enthusiasm one bit. I was raised in a larger household than mine now, and with only one bathroom so I knew this wasn't a problem whatsoever. I simply loved it. When I walked the children over for a look, they loved it too. When I showed Dad the house, he said, "Cheryl, I built this house thirty years ago." I knew right then why I loved the house so. Dad was an excellent carpenter. His completed work showed that he had poured his whole heart and soul into his works. I told him, "Dad, I should have known that your hands had laid this foundation because it is so beautiful." He just smiled and smiled. I could tell dad was excited about my buying this house as well. So it was settled. The Lord would bless us with this house, someway, somehow and I began to thank Him in advance for all of His tender mercies and blessings.

I continued to stay in close contact with my realtor. I had no idea what to expect when buying a house but I didn't know it could be so nerve racking. When finally, my credit was up to par and I had been approved for the loan, I had originally been told one figure which now turned into a whole different figure that I had to have for closing costs. I started to worry about it. Then, after asking God to work this seemingly monumental figure out for us, I made two phone calls. I called Evelyn and Doll. They were so happy and excited for me because they would tell me each time they visited me in the trailer that I really needed a house. Later when we talked about my little trailer, they both told me that they would actually be afraid of falling through the floors in the trailer. We were able to laugh about it, but at the time, there was nothing funny about it. Anyway, they each gave me the rest of the money I needed for the house and I can't thank them enough, even now. So, with dad right by my side at the lawyer's office, the same ones that had taken care of my divorce earlier, I sat there signing the closing papers and smiling like someone that had just hit the lottery for a million dollars. After this was over and I had the keys to my new home, dad carried me over to the house. The people that owned the home before me were very sweet people. They left a lot of nice furniture for me. They even left a bedroom, completely furnished. I decided that this would be for Cherylyn. I wanted to repay her for having to sleep on the sofa or to share the one tiny bedroom with her three brothers for all of the years she had to. She was thrilled. The boys were thrilled too. Boobie, for the very first time since he was in high school, invited some of his friends over. I was so proud and happy, I think for my children more than for myself. Michael, who loved water and fishing, was pleased with the house too. In the back of the house was a river. Michael would go to the back of the house and just sit there and watch the running water for hours on end. He later told me this relaxed him. It really was the only time I can remember Michael being still for that length of time. He could go fishing anytime he wanted to so all in all, we were very happy. We still had to walk everywhere we went, but thank God, we finally had a home. Vee again came through for me too. She went out of her way to pick me up for work and bring me back home from work. I was eventually able to put the car in the shop and it would run on again, off again, but I made up my mind that I would not complain about the car or anything else. I was too blessed to be stressed.

Chapter 33

It was Father's day and I had just come home from visiting Tobias. I was planning to take dad out to dinner that evening. My cousin called me and said, "You need to go to the hospital and check on your daddy. I think he had a stroke in church." Well, I was frozen stiff for a moment. As soon as I regained some kind of composure, I thanked her and instructed the children to stay inside and off to the hospital I rushed. When I arrived, I went looking for dad. I found him in the intensive care unit. He was lying there in bed and he was talking plain as day. He looked pretty good actually. I said, "Dad, what in the world happened? If you didn't wanna go out for dinner, you should have told me." He just smiled. Then he said, "I was preaching and the next thing I knew, I felt dizzy and passed out." I said, "Well, you need to hurry up and get out of here. We've all had enough of hospitals for a long while." He just smiled.

Sure enough, dad was discharged home about a week later. I noticed that he was weak but I attributed this to his being in the hospital for the longest time I can ever remember. I thought that lying down in bed for a week certainly contributed to his weakness. As days went by, he continued to go to the hospital for breakfast and fellowship but he just wasn't himself somehow. I called Evelyn and Doll and discussed dad's present situation with them. I told them, "I feel sorry for dad but I can't take him in to live with me and I can't go to live with him. I just purchased this house and my children are finally happy in their home. Dad and I have never gotten along anyway and I don't feel like hearing him fuss and preach to me and the children if I don't have to." They each fully understood, so it was decided. I would continue to check on dad everyday and invite him over for meals but I knew I did not want to live with him again.

One morning on the way from work, I detoured from my usual route. I drove past dad's house and I saw him parking his van. I slowed so as to observe him more closely. As he got out of the van, I noticed that he was very, very unsteady on his feet. It looked like he would take one step forward and three backward. That was it for me. I knew that I would not leave dad alone to take care of himself in this condition. In my mind, it was settled then and there. I would take dad into our home and the children and I would take care of him; that is if he would be in agreement with it. I immediately drove up in his driveway and I said, "Dad, you're coming to live with us." To my surprise he said, "Okay Cheryl." I tried to always discuss important decisions with Tobias beforehand but this was an emergency. Nonetheless, when Tobias called later that day, I told him what happened and what I wanted to do. Tobias, with his very sweet, caring, understanding self said, "Cheryl, that's a great idea." Tobias has always been very concerned and caring where family is concerned and this character in him only made me love him more and more. So,

it was settled, dad would move with us. I told the children
and they didn't say a word. I also talked with dad and I said,
"Dad, you're so welcomed in our home but please remember
that it is our home. The children and I are going to do everything in our power to make you as comfortable as possible
because we love you. All I ask is that you respect our privacy
and we'll do the same for you." I was looking for a powerful,
verbal response, one only dad could give. I was very surprised
when dad, as humbly as I've ever seen him said, "I'll respect
that and I thank you." So, Orlando packed dad's bedroom furniture and his favorite recliner in the truck and moved them
over to my house. The living room, which was a very sunny,
friendly room, my favorite in the whole house, was where I
decided I would convert to dad's bedroom. It was very spacious as well and I felt dad would enjoy it. So, Cherylyn and I
set about making dad's bedroom comfortable for him with his
favorite pictures of mom and him hanging on the wall. Dad
kept going on and on saying "I want David to come and get
my clocks and my bank books." I called David to tell him of
Dad's unusual request. Sure enough, David came down from
Northern Virginia and took dad's clocks and all of his banking
information back with him. Once this was done, dad seemed
very content.

I don't know how I would have made it without the help
of my children. I did not feel comfortable showering dad so
every morning before school, Tyrone Jr. as he now requested
everyone call him, took care of dad for me. He even shaved
him as well as a fifteen year old could. Michael and John Lee
brought him ice cream and juices to enjoy as he sat in his favorite recliner and watched the news. Malcolm, who was just
a year and a half, would come over to the recliner and ever
so lightly stroke dad's hand. Dad loved this and he'd just sit

there and smile. I was still leaving for work at six thirty in the evenings so Cherylyn would make sure dad ate supper and help him with his night clothes and tuck him in to bed every night. I thank God so much for my children. I simply could not have cared for dad alone. Orlando would come over in the evenings when he was sure I was at work. The children would tell me that Uncle O as they called him would come over and complain that dad was not shaved well or he was in the room or the house all alone. It's funny though. I cannot think of one time Orlando came over to assist with helping to bathe or shave dad or even bring him anything to eat or a cup of water to drink so I instructed the children to simply not open the door for him when he came. Because of Orlando's well-known short temper, the children would continue to open the door for him when he came over, out of fear I suppose. I continued to ignore Orlando and do the best that I could for dad. God knew my children and I were doing our best so it really didn't matter what anyone else thought.

Making ends meet was even more challenging now with a newly added member to the family. I called David on several occasions asking him to send some money for food for dad and money for his insurance premium. I told him that the insurance agent had been calling and calling and I simply did not have the money to pay it. My car was again, parked but I had dad's van. I used his van to purchase groceries and to take dad to his doctor's appointments, otherwise, I left the van parked and walked to work or rode with Vee. I did this because I knew Orlando would have a lot to say and I simply didn't want to hear it. I called Evelyn and Doll and told them that dad's health status was declining. He always loved to eat and now, his appetite was slowly dwindling. I prepared foods that I knew dad would love, and he would start off eating very well but would quickly seem to loose his appetite. One day, dad said "Cheryl, I want three spots" meaning fish, "I want them split down the center and fried lightly on each side." I was thrilled that finally his appetite was calling for something he liked. My spirits lifted as I drove to the store and purchased him the "three spots", the prettiest ones that I could find. I hurried home to prepare them just as he wanted. As I sat him down to the table, he seemed to enjoy the fish but he only ate one. I was really troubled then. Dad was beginning to hallucinate as well. When I would come home from work in the mornings, he would tell me, "That girl right there" meaning Cherylyn, "took my car and wrecked it. The police came and told me so." I would try to reassure him by telling him the van was in the driveway unharmed. I even took him to the door and showed him the van. He still was not convinced. Even in his weakened state, he still pulled off that Zoro belt a few times at Cherylyn, Michael and John Lee. They said he did actually swing it at them a few times but when it made contact, it didn't hurt at all. He stayed on Cherylyn's case so much until one morning when I came home, she was very upset. She said, "Momma, I don't think Grandpa loves me anymore. He's always accusing me of things I don't do." I explained to her that dad was imagining things and he's always loved her and he loves her now, he's just sick. This made her feel better. When he wasn't imagining things, he would always talk about the Lord. He didn't desire to go to church any longer but his church family came to visit him often. He seemed happy to see them whenever they came. He would often say, "I'm so glad I lived right." Dad was really getting weaker. He was not eating and he was incontinent as well. My brand new home smelled of urine, especially in his bedroom but I didn't mind at all. I just scrubbed and cleaned up his little accidents as he made them and went right along.

It had been three weeks since I asked David to send money for dad's insurance but he never did. Somehow, God blessed me with the money. The life insurance would lapse on Monday and I called the agent over to the house and paid him on that very Monday. I noticed dad was not getting any better and I knew that he would need his insurance paid, just in case. After taking care of that business, I called his doctor. I told him that dad was getting weak and not eating. He told me to bring him in. For some strange reason, this morning, I decided to bathe dad myself. I gave him a bubble bath from head to toe and shaved him. As we were standing in the tiny little bathroom and I was drying dad off, he leaned over to me and gave me the most gentle, little, weak, wet kiss on my cheek. This surprised me. Then he said, "Cheryl, I didn't think you would treat me like this." I replied, "Dad, how did you think I would treat you?" I already knew why he thought I would mistreat him but my heart would never have let me do that. After much wrestling to get him dressed and in the van, we finally made it to the hospital where he was immediately admitted. On Monday afternoon, dad was talking and I had never seen him so sweet and peaceful as now. I thought, maybe he just needs some fluids to hydrate him and he'll be good as new. Dad had always been in the best of health. I went to work feeling encouraged. On Tuesday, the doctor told me to call all the family together and I was totally baffled. "Dad's doing better" I argued. The doctor just told me to go to check on him. When I arrived in dad's room, there he lay in and out of consciousness. I immediately left and went over to Orlando's house. I didn't know how upset I was but when Orlando opened the door, I just started screaming and crying. I said,

"You have to come back to the hospital with me because I can't do this by myself anymore, I just can't." He saw how upset I was and he came back with me to the hospital. When we went into dad's room, dad lay there with his eyes closed. Orlando said to him, "Dad, who am I?" Dad responded, "You're David." So I asked him, "Dad, who am I?" I'll never forget his response. He started smiling and smiling and said, "You're Cheryl." That response made me feel real good.

Chapter 34

It was Wednesday, two days after I took dad to the hospital. He was comatose now. If he knew any of us were there, we didn't know it. I had called all of my sisters and brothers to come home as instructed by dad's doctor. I remember I was working the 3-11 shift this day and my brother David and his wife had arrived at the hospital. I was standing in the hallway talking to Lydia, David's wife, when I heard the most disturbing noise. I was not an intensive care nurse but I knew the sound of this monitor did not sound just right. As I ran to the nurse's station, I was cornered by a very sweet nurse named Cindy. She said, Cheryl, he's gone. I just started hugging her very tightly. Finally, when I let her go, she said, "Go in and say your goodbyes." I went stumbling in the room. Dad looked so peaceful lying there still with a smile on his face. I don't know exactly how I felt. I remember feeling very alone and empty inside. I had just lost mom nine months earlier and now dad. I just wanted with all my heart for Tobias to be able to be here with me, for me, and to reassure me that everything would be alright. At this very moment, I felt weak. I was so

tired of facing anything, everything all alone. Queeta came
from the OB department and hugged me and tried to comfort
me as she walked me back to my department. There were all
of the nurses, friends as I had come to label them, standing
there waiting to comfort me. Finally Vee said, "Now Cheryl,
you're a strong woman, God made you strong and you have
to display that strength now more than ever. You have to be
strong for your sisters and brothers and your children." I just
stood there thinking, "Who will be my strength? I've had to
be strong for everyone else for as long as I can remember. Do
I count?" Nonetheless, I knew Vee was right. So, I managed
to stop crying and pull myself together. As I drove home I remember thanking God for blessing me with the money to pay
dad's life insurance policy. I also remember being so glad that
I decided to take dad into our home and care for him. If it had
not been for that one month out of my life, I might never have
felt that dad really did love me. I suppose he had to be hard
core and strict. At the age of fourteen, his mother died leaving
his dad, his three siblings and him alone. He was forced to
quit school in the seventh grade, as much as he loved learning,
to work and take care of his younger brothers and a sister and
had been working every since. I suppose he had to develop a
hard nosed attitude.

I got the children and brought them back to the hospital to
say their last goodbyes. Tyrone Jr. was tearful but he remained
strong for his sister and brothers. Cheryln was downright
pitiful. She cried and cried, all the while hugging dad's neck
tightly. She didn't want to let go of him. Despite dad's fussing
and beating them, they still loved him and were very close
to him. After some time, I gathered the children and we rode
home in silence.

It seemed that we had just gone through this ritual a few

days ago, not nine months ago, yet here we sat again in that same funeral parlor, discussing the same things. We decided that everyone would be received at my home now, something that I was not looking forward to in the least. I managed to sit there smiling at all the guests as they poured in and out of the house. Again, everyone was really sweet and tried to say encouraging words to the family. I thank God that again, my mother-n-law came down from Northern Virginia to show support for me and my family. On the day of the funeral, we again formed a line in cars and rode slowly and silently to the same church, the one that many years earlier, dad and mom built. During the service, a group of elders sang a song that was composed by none other than dad himself. We the children were quite surprised and impressed. We knew dad loved to read and study but we never knew he was a composer of music. He was full of surprises indeed. It was a very nice song too. The funeral, to my surprise and appreciation didn't last as long as the traditional holiness funeral normally lasts. We all viewed dad for our last time and afterward, we went to lay him to rest right beside mom. I was sad but I didn't feel as sad because I knew within my heart that I had done my very best for dad. I loved my dad so much. He was my very best friend when I was a little girl. He was a good father too, despite his fussing, giving you the beatings of your life, and being super strict, as I reflected back on my childhood. We had a very nice, comfortable home that he designed and constructed with his own hands. There was always plenty of good food to eat. We always wore nice clothes and we got everything we wanted at Christmastime. As we got older, we would order our own toys from the Sears and Roebuck catalog. We could charge it to dad's accounts and never hear anything more about it. We could go to stores and just say, "Charge it to John Lee White

Sr.'s account". It was as easy as that. Dad always paid the bills for whatever we charged. The electricity, water, telephone was always on, never, ever had it been off. I realized now, sitting here a grown woman myself with a family, just how hard providing for a family really is. It was even harder back in the days when dad had to do it and he did a terrific job. He didn't have to stay with a woman with six children if he didn't really love us and want to but he did. Most importantly, the last thirty days that I spent with my dad was a blessing right from God. We grew close again and I was reassured that he did indeed love me. For the past eighteen years, Doll had been asking me to move away from our small hometown. I never wanted to even though she was right about all the reasons that I should have. I just never wanted to leave mom and dad for reasons that I myself didn't even realize or understand. Now I know that it was not my doing but that of God. He knew my parents would need somebody and He had already chosen me.

Later back at the house, John Lee, Jr, Orlando, David, Evelyn, Doll and myself sat down to discuss what was to be done with dad and mom's house and belongings since Dad had left no will. Doll and Evelyn immediately said, "We want Cheryl to keep the van because she really needs it for her and her children." Well this idea was not the right one. My brothers Orlando and David said, "We've already decided that John Lee will take the van back with him to New Jersey." Evelyn and Doll were angry. They protested, all to no avail. This had already been decided and that was that. I didn't say anything one way or another. I knew that I was no stranger to walking where I needed to go and I knew that the van was dads, not mine anyway.

I couldn't recall what real contributions Orlando and David made while mom and dad were ailing but I certainly saw them in action once they were dead. One morning bright and early, David drove down with his truck and an attachment for carrying more things secured on the back of the truck. Aunt Rae was in Virginia as well on this particular day. Aunt Rae went over to dad's house to see just what was going on. There she witnessed Orlando and David gathering everything of our parents that they wanted, the riding lawn mower, all of the tools, the printer, fax machine, whatever. Orlando's girlfriend Dee was trying on mom's furs and hats and Aunt Rae was furious. She called me and told me to come over there and see what was going on but I had no desire to do so, and I told her just that. I said, "Aunt Rae, none of that stuff belongs to me, it was moms and dads. I'm not about to come over there and get into a fight with Orlando about it because you know that's exactly what would happen." She understood and didn't say anything more about it. Sometime that afternoon, Orlando and/or David came over and placed a cardboard box on my back porch. In it was a bunch of junk. There were some cans of food and a lot of mom's whatnots that she treasured so much along with some other stuff. The whatnots were mostly all broken though. I left the box on the porch and took out the intact whatnots and those that weren't broken so badly. Then I asked Tyrone Jr. to put the box and its remaining contents out on the street for the garbage men to dispose of because that is just what it was, garbage.

Chapter 35

Malcolm was growing so fast. He was a really good little boy too. Because his birthday came after September 1st, he couldn't go to pre-kindergarten the year that we thought he would. I think I was more upset than he was. Since he was three years old, he'd been saying, "Momma, I want to be a petricen when I grow up. If I make A's in school, can I grow my hair?" He was such a smart, intelligent little person. I guess he had to grow up fast being around older brothers and a sister. He went through a period where he cursed too. I think this came from being around older brothers and a sister as well. On weekends when we visited Tobias, I would tell him about Malcolm's cursing. He would sit Malcolm on his lap and say, "Now, daddy's man shouldn't say bad words okay? It's not nice so you're daddy's main man and you can't do or say bad things, okay?" Malcolm would sit there on his daddy's lap and look all innocent with the big old puppy dog looking eyes and shake his head up and down in agreement. Just as soon as we'd leave the prison and go to a store or wherever, Malcolm would start up again. This went on for a few months. I was really glad when he grew out of that phase. Anyway, I went to the school to speak with a very sweet lady, Dr. Lea. I wanted to see if there was anything that could be done about this birthday after September rule. She sympathized with me and told me that there was nothing that could be done about Malcolm's birthday but there was plenty that I could do that would more than prepare him for pre-k for the following year. I thank her to this day for all of the activities and ideas she shared with me that made learning fun. I wish I had known these things with all of the children. My dad always said, "A child's mind is like a blank sheet of paper. It's up to us what we write on it." That is so very true. It is so vitally important to teach our children very good things at a very early age. It means the world to them and us as they grow older.

Tobias' dad never called us, wrote us, or anything else. I felt that if I had a grandson that I'd never seen, I would surely be interested in knowing something about him. Since Walt did not take the initiative to see, or even ask about Malcolm, I took it upon myself to take Malcolm and the rest of the children to visit him. I was very proud of my children and I wanted Walt to see what a fine son, through God, Tobias had made. So, we all drove to see Mother and Walt. They both were remarried but they didn't live very far from each other. When we arrived, I wanted to visit Walt. I wanted to see how he received Malcolm. Tobias' sister and her two children, along with me and Malcolm went over to his house. I don't know what my first impression of him was but Malcolm warmed up to him immediately. Our visit wasn't long. We talked a little bit and took some pictures. Before we left, Walt promised to keep in contact with us. That would prove to be a very empty promise.

My days at the hospital changed but I was still working midnights. I would now work during the week so that I had every other weekend off. In the mornings when I came home from work, I would see the children on the school bus. Then I would bathe and dress Malcolm, prepare his breakfast and afterward, I would instruct him to watch Sesame Street, not open the door for anyone and I placed finger foods out for him. I would then lie down on the sofa in the den as Malcolm sat there cross-legged on the floor in front of the television watching all his favorite shows and singing along, counting, whatever as I napped off and on. When I got up sometime midday, I would prepare lunch and after eating together, we would work on the activities that Dr. Lea shared with me earlier. That was our daily routine. Everyday before the children came home; I cooked a full course meal. Tyrone Jr. would sometimes ask, "Momma how is it that you can cook a full meal including desserts, even when it doesn't look like we've got much food?" I'd just look at him and smile. I knew that it wasn't any doing of my own, that's for sure.

I decided to go to work for a home health agency. I had my car repaired and it was holding up pretty well this time so I wasn't afraid to travel distances. On weekends, I would start out very early to go out to places that I didn't even know existed. I would try to visit four to five patients both on Saturday and Sunday. On those weekend nights that I worked, I would leave from work in the mornings and head to the home health jobs before coming home to bathe, spend some time with the children, cook and get some sleep. I was never a daytime sleeper because daylight was when everything else needed to be done, or so I felt. I'd be somewhat rest broken but I managed this crazy schedule anyway by God's grace and mercy. I loved home health nursing as well. I got to meet and visit with really nice patients in their homes. Most of them were able to move around, but some of them were bedridden. I met a lot of nice families and gave good care at the same time. Sometimes during the childrens' school holidays, I would do some home visits as well. This second job proved to be quite a blessing. I was able to buy better clothes and sneakers for all of my babies and I was happy about that. Cherylyn would later tease me saying "I never wore a pair of name brand sneakers until I was in Jr. High." I said, "At least momma kept some shoes on your feet, you weren't barefooted." We would just laugh. Tyrone Jr. was in his senior year and he was working as well. He was always a very smart guy and he loved to work and make his own money. Tobias was helping to supplement our income as well. He had taken up the trade of working with leather and he made some of the most beautiful pocketbooks, belts and wallets I've ever seen. His style was very unique. His very first work, which was a very nice pocketbook, he gave to me. Tobias had become famous for doing very sweet, thoughtful things that made me feel like a teenager again. He knew just what to do and to say to make me blush and feel all mushy inside. Though not a day went by that I didn't miss or think about mom and dad, I only had to think about something Tobias said or did and I would immediately go into my little comfort, satisfied zone.

In June, at the age of sixteen, Tyrone Jr. graduated from high school. I was one proud mom for sure. Despite all of the obstacles this little family had been through, Tyrone Jr. managed to do well in school and finish one year early. Right after graduation, he said, "Momma, I want to join the Army. I called the recruiter and he's coming over to meet us this afternoon." Well, I was speechless for a moment. Then I said, "Tyrone Jr., you've never been away from home or your family. Are you sure this is what you want to do?" He had obviously given a lot of thought to this idea and he said he was sure. So, that afternoon, the recruiter came over and talked with the both of us. Tyrone Jr. passed the entrance test with no problem. Soon after that, my baby, my firstborn, my right-hand man was taken by the recruiter to a hotel in Richmond to wait to be flown to basic training.

Michael continued to have trouble focusing in school. He was an extremely intelligent, bright student but he had trouble paying attention and being quiet once his work in school was done. I finally decided to try the Ritalin therapy. I observed Michael when I gave it to him. He was still into everything and remained very busy and mischievous. The only difference I noticed was that he was losing weight because he was not eating well. He wasn't sleeping as well either. I really didn't want to continue with this medicine but I did. I thought that once it was in his system really well, it would begin to make a difference. Tobias and I had discussed Michael on many occasions and we both felt that his main problem was not having his father show any interest in him. Tobias felt that he needed a structured kind of discipline as well. So, I started to look into military academies for him because I so much wanted to help him. Every one of the programs that I contacted was very expensive. The least expensive one costs more than my mortgage payments per month. There was no way I could afford that. I felt so very helpless. I wanted so desperately to help my child but I didn't know how best to do it. I asked the school if they would recommend some good places that I could take Michael so he could learn to focus and get on track. They gave me some listings of group homes. When I heard the word group home, I was immediately turned off. The counselor assured me that these were good homes that could help troubled boys. "That is what they specialize in" I was told by the counselor. So, after discussing this with Tobias, we decided to give it a try at least.

I reluctantly met with the director of this group home. The home was on the outskirts of Richmond. After talking with the staff there and looking around, touring the place, I decided that I would try this for Michael. It was based on my income too, so I knew I could pay for his expenses. I would just work a little more if I had to. Michael needed help. That was that.

So, in the middle of Michael's sixth grade year, I took him to this group home. Inside were boys of all ages, or so it looked to me. As I walked around looking at Michael's new environment, I learned that a lot of these boys didn't even have parents, mother or father and I immediately thought, "Michael's situation is so different. He has a mother and a step-father who adore him. He has a sister that has practically raised him and brothers who adore him. Oh God, am I doing the right thing?" I brought Michael's Ritalin with us as well and the name of our doctor just in case they needed him. When it was time for me to go, I left Michael with a room full of strangers that day. As I walked to the car, my heart felt as though it were too big for my chest. My feet felt like they weighed one hundred pounds each. I cried all the way back home.

I called the group home almost every day. Every weekend after visiting Tobias, we would go to the Group Home to visit Michael. He seemed to be adjusting just fine. I always baked a cake or cookies to bring with me and Michael and the other boys just loved this. Michael was doing very well in the school there too. They went on very nice field trips and things seemed to be going well. Then, one night at home lying in bed, the telephone rang. It was the Home. The counselor was telling me that Michael had run away. I kept asking where he was and what happened to cause him to run away? The counselor wouldn't give me any direct answers. I asked him if anyone had gone to look for him. He said, "We don't look for them when they run off, they'll eventually come back." Well, all I could think about was my eleven year old out somewhere at night on the streets of Richmond, running around upset and all alone. I told the counselor that I would be over in about two hours. He talked and talked and was finally able to talk me out of it. He assured me that this type of thing happened all the time and the boys always came back. Sure enough, about an hour later, the counselor called and told me Michael was back. I asked to speak with him so that I could hear his voice for myself. Michael sounded very upset when he picked up the telephone. I said, "Sweetie Pie, what on earth has gotten you so upset that you ran away?" He simply said, "Momma, I'm tired of everything." This response really did alarm me. "Oh God, oh God, I'm so very tired of going through everything all by myself. I need Tobias here with me so that I can lean on his shoulders. I need some help Lord. I know you're here with me God and I know you'll never leave me, but I need Tobias here physically with me." That is all I kept saying as I cried myself to sleep that night.

It had been six months since I took Michael to the home for boys. When checking with his counselors, there was not much difference in Michael. He remained hyperactive. The only difference I could see myself was his obvious weight loss. I drove over before the school year started again, and I picked him up and brought him home, much to the counselor's dismay. Once we arrived home, I enrolled Michael in regular public school. I couldn't see where making the drastic decision of placing him in the boy's home really helped him. The only thing I noticed was that where Michael was just mischievously busy before being away from home, now he had a lot of new found knowledge and none of it seemed good to me. He had been around a lot of boys from different kinds of lifestyles and he had learned a lot of disruptive behaviors. What a horrible mistake I had made taking him in the first place. It's such a shame that hindsight is 20/20.

Tyrone Jr. was graduating from basic training that fall. I, the children and my old trusty car drove to St. Louis to see Tyrone Jr.'s graduation. I was so proud of him. My heart felt too big for my chest at that moment. The whole ceremony seemed rushed to me. After graduation, we were rushed into a building where we had a rushed meal with our soldier, and then we were rushed to say our goodbyes and then the graduates were rushed onto buses to be taken to AIT or advanced individual training. After all of this whirlwind ceremony was finished, the children and I headed back on the long, twenty four hour drive home.

After completing AIT, Tyrone Jr. decided to come back home and join the National Guard. I asked him why he didn't join the regular Army so that he could travel and see some far away places. He smiled and said, "Mom, I just want to stay around here for a while and work." He was only seventeen years old so I didn't say anything more about it. He found a job and eventually rented a house. He was always a very independent guy. He started living with a girl that I saw as a very nice girl and they both seemed happy enough. He went to drill once a month and two weeks in the summer. He seemed very content with his decision so I was too.

Michael was doing a lot better in regular public school. He was a grade behind and he wanted so much to play basketball. The counselor and his teachers gave him a chance to make up all missed work and in one semester, Michael completed all of his work and was placed in his regular grade. He was so proud of himself and so was I. He tried out for the basketball team and he made it. He not only made the team, he was in

the first five of the starting line up. Michael was such an excit-
ing player to watch. He was a natural at sports and basketball was no different. We, meaning myself, Cherylyn, John Lee
and Malcolm went to every game, home and away. My newly
discovered son Terry came to see Michael play too. Tyrone Jr.
came to a lot of the home games as well. Michael was an awe-
some player and he was one of the leading scorers. He made
lots of assists too. It was a really great season. After the season,
at the banquet, Michael was chosen Co-MVP and received
honors and a nice trophy. I was so proud of him at that very
moment. I had taken him off of the Ritalin and I figured I'd just
keep him very busy with sports and any other positive thing
that I could think of. He'd be too tired to get into anything else.
Even though I had one outlook for Michael's life, he had an entirely different one. He hung around a lot of boys and I didn't
like any of them. They were boys who could hang out in the
streets and do whatever they wanted to, when they wanted
to. I was not raising Michael like that but it seemed the more I
protested, the worse things got. My working long hours didn't
help matters either.

It had gotten so that almost every weekend I visited Tobias, he would tell me to follow Tyrone Jr. and watch what's
he's getting into. I would ask him why he said that. He would
tell me that he's been hearing that Tyrone Jr. had been getting
into some things that if not stopped, just might land him in
prison. I was very alarmed. So I asked Tyrone Jr. what he was
into. He just looked at me and said, "Momma, I don't know
why Tobias told you that. I'm doing just fine. I'm not into anything but working, some partying and coming home." I knew
that my plate was already quite full with being full-time mom
and dad, working two jobs and keeping track of Michael so it
would have been virtually impossible for me to play detective

where Tyrone Jr. was concerned anyway. I'd never had any trouble with him before so I began to think that perhaps whoever was telling Tobias these things might have meant Tyrone Sr., not Tyrone Jr.

Chapter 36

It seemed that Tobias was in and out of segregation a lot. He was frequently the focus of the administration for one reason or another. It was emotionally straining enough to visit him in the prison environment where our every word, every gesture was closely monitored. Whenever he was in segregation, I had to visit him in a separate building and a glass partition separated us and we had to talk on a telephone. Talk about being impersonal. The children were so used to playing with him, wrestling with him, listening to his lectures, just interacting with him period. They didn't like seeing him in segregation either. Tobias, this time, had been in segregation for almost a year, or so it seemed. Finally, I had a very serious discussion with him. I said, "Tobias is this how you're going to live in here for the time you're here? I know you say you love us but I'm really not convinced that you mean it. When you're in segregation, you risk loosing any good time that you've earned and you also run the risk of prolonging your prison sentence. Is this what you want? If not, you must show me that you want me and you want to be with me and this family." Show me is exactly what Tobias did. After this last bout of segregation, Tobias became focused on staying out of it. Whatever had happened to cause undue focus on Tobias was now turned around. Now, he was getting a lot of attention from the officers in the form of commendation letters. Whenever there was any kind of trouble brewing between inmates, the officers would ask Tobias to intervene. Tobias was also instrumental in working with the younger inmates on their academics. He took them under his wings and tutored them. He helped quite a few to study for and obtain their GED. He helped the older inmates with basic things that the older men found hard to do like writing letters for them. He also assisted the older inmates with things as menial as dressing themselves. Tobias was a jewel in my eyes for sure. I was so very proud of him. I loved him even more too for the love and dedication he showed this family. I can only imagine how difficult prison life must be but Tobias was determined to turn it around and make the best out of it and he did. What's more, he did it mostly out of love for me and the children. He would often say, "Cheryl, you and the children reached out to me when my own family seemed to have forgotten about me. You're all the family I have." Family was indeed important to Tobias. We all were proud of Tobias and he was proud of himself as well. He sent home copies of his commendation letters. These letters went on to say things like:

To Whom It May Concern:

Mr. Tobias entered the Painting/Drywall class in June and graduated in February. He was an excellent student and was very instrumental in helping other students with both their class work and hands-on physical skills. As a result of his behavior, I selected him to be a teacher's aide. He has done an outstanding job assisting students in their work and assisting me with the maintenance of various reports-monthly, annual and periodic student progress reports for each student. He has not only increased his skills relating to this vocation but has learned to operate the computer programs required to maintain the records of the students. He is computer literate using Microsoft Word, Excel and some Access. He has a very positive behavior and is a stable influence in this class. He gets along well with everyone.

Another commendation letter said:

To Whom It May Concern:

In the past two and a half years that I've know Inmate Tobias, I cannot recall a time when I've had to seriously issue this inmate an order to stop violating any of the institutional rules or regulations. It is because of this inmate's good character that I did not hesitate to write this letter on Inmate Tobias' behalf. In any prison environment there will be inmates who are opposite of the majority of other prisoners. Inmate Tobias is one of those prisoners. In talking with this particular inmate from time to time, I can tell that he tries to improve himself each day, and more often than not he does so by helping other inmates learn to read and write. Inmate Tobias has a very strong but quiet confidence about himself and even the most incorrigible inmates listen to him when he speaks. The relationship with staff that Inmate Tobias has is rooted in courtesy, respect, and strict adherence to the rules of this institution while leading by example the way that the younger inmates should follow. Whatever Inmate Tobias has done in the past, he certainly appears to have put it all behind him, and he seems relentlessly focused on the ultimate goal of getting out and starting over.

These were just a few of the numerous letters of commendation that Tobias received.

Later, with documentation that Tobias was able to mail to me, I saw that the administrative holds were, in the end and for the most part, unsubstantiated allegations. The department of corrections does not look favorably on relationships/ marriages between co-workers and inmates. I knew this from all of the mean statements made to me by some of the employees there, the few that knew of me and the majority that did not. I really didn't mind them saying or doing mean things to me but when it involved my children, that was another matter altogether. Cherylyn was in the tenth grade. She came home very upset one afternoon. She was crying and said she had been for most of the day. After asking her what happened she said, "We had this substitute teacher today. He works at the prison too. For the entire class period, he kept asking me why my mother married an inmate and how in the world she had a baby by an inmate." I was livid. The next morning, I called the principal, Mrs. Yong. She had been in the school system for a long time. She had been my older brothers and sisters teacher as well as mine. One thing I can say about her is that she has always been fair and honest. She's been the same for the numerous years that I've known her, even to her style of dress and how she wore her hair. Anyway, I told her my concerns and she scheduled a meeting with this substitute and me for the next morning. Once we were all seated in her office, she began by saying, "The one thing I am going to demand here and now is respect. Neither of you will say anything derogatory about the other." I had grown up in the same town with this man and I had never done anything to him to make him say anything out of the way to me, much less my child. I had never even paid him any attention as a matter of fact. Anyway, we both complied with Mrs. Yong's wishes. Thus, the conference started. She asked me what had made Cherylyn so upset in class. I told her that Mr. Taylor had chosen to question and cross-examine her in class for the entire period instead of doing what he was being paid to do, direct the classroom in instruction in the absence of the teacher. I told the both of them that my personal life had no business in the classroom setting and my life was none of his business. I went on to say that if he ever substituted for any one of my children again, it would be to his advantage to conduct himself as a substitute teacher, not my personal life advisor. When Mr. Taylor was given a chance to speak, his question to me was, "Were you fired from the prison or did you resign?" I knew right then and there that I was talking with a fool and my mama always said, "You cannot reason with a fool." My dad had a saying as well. It was, "It is better to remain silent and be thought a fool than to open your mouth and remove all doubt." I answered his question and told him that I had given my two week resignation per protocol. Mrs. Yong didn't say anything more. I think she was thinking the same thing that I, at that moment, knew for sure. After that meeting, Cherylyn said that he never substituted anymore, at least not at her school. So many occurrences happened with some of the staff of the Department of Corrections (DOC) and me until I never doubted Tobias' views of them again. After really delving into some of the reasons that a charge could be written up on an inmate, which brings about some sort of reprimand in the prison system, Tobias explained to me that having your hair too long or having one too many tee shirts or underwear could constitute a charge being written on you by an officer. In Tobias' case, the officers seemed to pay extra attention to him all of the time. He said this was not the case until after our marriage. I surely was not aware that I was such an important point of interest until I married Tobias. I remember thinking, "If they're going to be all up in our business, I wish they would take over the financial aspect of my business and pay my bills."

It was late summer when I received a telephone call from Tobias. He seemed to be concerned which made me concerned. He said, "Sweetheart, I'm just calling you to let you know that I think a riot is about to happen and I just want to assure you that I'm not involved in any way. I don't want you to worry about anything. My cell mate and I are going to remain in our cells. I just wanted to let you know what was going on while I had a chance because I don't want you to worry." Then he hung up. I did feel better knowing that Tobias could not be looked at by the administration for this and I felt reasonably sure that no harm would come to him if he were locked in his cell. Sure enough, the entire prison population was placed on lockdown. Nothing more was said about this riot. Then, in February of the next year, Tobias says an officer came to his cell and handcuffed him and ordered Tobias to come with him. When Tobias asked the reason for this, he was given a detention form that stated "For participating in an unauthorized and/or group demonstration." Tobias denied this because he knew he had been in his cell with his cellmate the entire time this disturbance was going on months earlier. His cell mate was not handcuffed either and nothing was said to his cellmate. Nonetheless, Tobias had to appear before the ICC

(Institutional Classification Committee) as it was known then. A Psychologist named Mr. McKine chaired this committee. Tobias said Mr. McKine told him that he was brought before this committee for receiving over nine infractions within a twelve month period and for his involvement in the recent institutional disturbance. Tobias said he then asked Mr. McKine to name and date each of the alleged charges but Mr. McKine declined to do so. Instead, Mr. McKine went on to say that Tobias had been positively identified by an officer via videotaping during this prison disturbance. Well Tobias became angry and called Mr. McKine a liar and told him that each time he chaired an ICC hearing or even been a member of a committee that Tobias had been brought before, Tobias ended up in segregation based on unsubstantiated allegations. Tobias also told him that it was impossible for the officer to videotape him unless he videotaped him in his cell where he remained after notifying his wife of the disturbance. Nonetheless, Mr. McKine, speaking for all of the present committee members said, "The committee is inclined to believe the officer. Do you have anything else to say before this committee renders its decision?" Tobias said he replied, "The chairman, not the committee seems to have his mind made up already so it doesn't matter what I say at this point." He says he was then ushered outside of the office for approximately one to one and a half minutes before he was brought back in. Then Mr. McKine says "It is the decision of the committee to place you in Custodial Management Segregation." Tobias says at that moment, he thought about all of the other times he had been placed in Segregation for bogus reasons and he completely lost it. He said he kicked the door open very hard, so hard that it hit the wall, slammed back and reopened. He said that there was another ICC committee meeting right across the hall in session. He said that the prisoner was agitated and everyone's attention was drawn to that room. He says that it was then that Mr. McKine knocked on the window right behind Tobias and gave him the middle finger and mouthed the words, "F you Nigger." Tobias said he then took one step back and kicked the window where Mr. McKine sat with his back turned as though he hadn't done a thing. The kick shattered the glass and Mr. McKine fell forward as though Tobias' foot had struck him in the back of his head. When the officers arrived, Mr. McKine grabbed the back of his head and told the officers that Tobias has assaulted him. Tobias was then escorted back to the security officer where he broke down in tears while speaking to another officer about what had just happened and what had been happening all along. Tobias was charged with Assault Upon Any Person, DOC offense code #105. He had to spend 15 days in isolation and the loss of 30 days of his good time. Tobias says for the next few months, he remained in D-unit, watching Mr. McKine come and go from D-unit.

At some point, Mr. McKine had Tobias served with a warrant for Simple Assault in the County of my small hometown. This man contended that Tobias had "struck me in the rear of my head thus causing tears in the retina of my right eye." He further asserted that the retinal tears progressed to complete retinal detachment and laser surgery and because of this, had been away from work since the incident. A very fair and smart attorney named Ms. Pearson was chosen to represent Tobias in court. The court date was scheduled for December 21st. Ms. Pearson had subpoenaed the entry logbook and adjustment committee tape which would prove beyond any doubt that Mr. McKine had in fact been working since the incident. Further, Ms. Pearson had been able to ascertain that Mr. McKine's eye care was done by or at a Retina Asociation office further north and she had obtained a copy of his medical record from there as well.

At the trial, Ms. Pearson requested that the witnesses be sequestered until each of them had been called in. The prosecutor called Mr. McKine who maintained that he had been assaulted by Tobias; that he had been away from work, and the seriousness of his injury was caused, according to his ophthalmologist, by the blow to the back of his head. Ms. Pearson then cross-examined him. She asked him if he was certain that Tobias' foot struck him in the rear of his head; was he certain that if Tobias' foot struck him, it was deliberate; how long had he been having trouble with his vision, etc. Mr. McKine was certain that Tobias' foot struck him, certain that it was deliberate, and that he'd been having trouble with his vision since approximately 2-3 weeks following the incident. Ms. Pearson then asked him where he had the eye surgery done. He said it was done at the Retina Association. Ms. Pearson then said, "And your doctor there is certain that this injury caused your retinal tear?" He answered, "Yes." Then Ms. Pearson asked, "And you had no serious vision problems before this incident with Mr. Tobias?" He answered, "No." Then Ms. Pearson said, "Then why does your doctor at the Retina Association inform me that not only have you had retinal tears before this incident but you've had diminishing vision problems for over 10 years!" Tobias says Mr. McKine was speechless. Ms. Pearson then said, "No further questions." Then Tobias said the other persons that were in the committee meeting that day were called in and soon it was very clear that nobody could say with any degree of certainty that Tobias had kicked Mr. McKine in the back of his head. The jury was out all of twenty minutes before returning with a Not Guilty verdict. Tobias says that as he was being escorted back to the van by security, Mr. McKine turned to him and said, "I'll personally see to it that you do every day of your sentence." When Tobias told me what Mr. McKine had said to him, I felt very down. Tobias said that he wondered how Mr. McKine could make such a statement as adamantly as he did and with such surety. Anyway, Tobias assured me that God would be the deciding factor, not Mr. McKine. I was still concerned though. I had been dealing with the Department of Corrections long enough now to know that whatever they said was just that and that the majority of them would stick together, at least over an inmate's word.

Chapter 37

Malcolm started kindergarten at last. Beforehand, he had to complete a series of tests. After these tests were concluded, he was labeled as gifted. I was so proud of him. He loved school and he absorbed everything the teacher taught him like a little sponge. I kept him active in after school activities as well so he would be a well-rounded little individual. He especially loved tee ball and we all enjoyed watching him play. No one could tell him he wasn't the next Jackie Robinson. John Lee was doing very well in school too. Both he and Malcolm were competitors at heart so they always did their best in school so as to be among the top students. Cherylyn was now in her senior year. She had the same problems as I did when I was going to school with girls picking on her. I was so glad that she was almost through with high school until I didn't know what to do. Michael was still running with the wrong boys and they were still putting him up to doing all kinds of crazy things. He would steal my bill money out of my wallet so that he could spend it on his girlfriends, his boys and weed. This hurt me to my heart. Then I remembered how much I hurt and worried my mom and this thought came to mind: "What goes around comes back around." Reaping what one sows and in double measures sure was a whole lot. I made up my mind right then and there that I would be extra conscious of how I treated people because I had reaped too many bad seeds. I was determined that my harvest would consist of good seeds from here on out. Anyway, Michael's acts ultimately ended him in the Juvenile system.

It was early summer, just before the new school year started. I knew that Michael needed to be kept busy so I went to talk to this man who owned a car repair shop. I pleaded with him to give Michael a job for the summer with him. I explained that I was having some problems with him and I felt he needed to be around a positive male influence and I thought this man would be just that. After some pondering, the man decided to give Michael a job. It was his first day on his new job and as I dropped him off, I felt that this might really be good for Michael. I came back home and told Cherylyn and John Lee to take care of Malcolm until I returned from the grocery store. When I returned home about an hour later, John Lee was crying. Cherylyn told me the police had come to the house while I was gone and was looking for Michael. John Lee told the policeman exactly where Michael was and they had gone to Michael's new job and picked him up and carried him to a juvenile facility in Petersburg. Talk about mad, not angry. I immediately went to the police station to find the policeman that had been to my house and questioned my minor children in my absence. They would not tell me very much but sent me to the Juvenile probation office. Seeing how very mad I was, I feel certain that someone at the police station called ahead to alert this Ms. Slate, the juvenile probation officer, of my pending arrival. When I reached the office, I was crying. I was so hurt and angry. It took forever for Ms. Slate to come out of her office to see me. When I threatened to go back on my own and find her, the receptionist told Ms. Slate what I said and she appeared, like magic, within a few minutes. Once in her office I asked her how it was that she could send a police officer to my home to question my minor children in my absence. Before she could think of a response, I fired a second question at her. I asked her how it was that she could authorize anyone to pick my minor son up and take him anywhere without my prior knowledge. She gave me some lame explanation but I could hardly focus on her. What I wanted to do at that very moment was trash that entire office with her in it. I had to really pray and ask God to give me a calm spirit, immediately. I left the office still very upset and tearful. Once I arrived back at home, I scolded John Lee real good. I told him that if he ever divulged any information on any family member ever again, I would skin his butt.

I went to work that evening and luckily for me, I was assigned to a patient that was in pre-term labor. This young lady was on a magnesium sulfate drip. This medicine tends to make one very sleepy and my patient slept the entire shift. After getting report, I pulled up a chair to my patient's bedside. I cannot say how I felt but I don't remember feeling much worse in life than at that moment. I cried and cried and cried silently that entire shift while monitoring her uterine and fetal activity. Vee came into the room and asked me what in the world was wrong. I could not even tell her, I just sit there looking down at my assessment sheet with the tears falling and falling. Vee was leaving work and as she left, she hugged me. I still was in my own little world. About an hour later a delivery came for me. Vee had gone by the floral shop and sent me the most beautiful bouquet of roses I had ever seen. The card was not signed but it had a very motivating message on it so I knew that she had sent it. I thanked God right then and there for sending Vee into my life. She'd been my shoulder on which to lean each time I was convinced I couldn't make it any further.

Michael ended up staying in this juvenile facility for a couple of months I think. He was the platoon leader and seemed to do excellent under direct supervision. I learned from going to his trial that he had stolen some items from one of our neighbor's homes. This neighbor had been a very sweet man to Michael and had invited him into his home and this was the thanks he received. I was very disappointed in Michael. Nonetheless, I hung in there with him. After being released, I enrolled Michael in high school. He tried out for the football team and had secured a position as one of the quarterbacks. I was so proud of him. Then, the counselor, Mrs. DeLow, informed me that Michael was missing some of his required state tests so he couldn't play football until that was completed. I asked her that since she was his counselor, shouldn't she have know this prior to the start of the football season and made me aware of it? She didn't seem apologetic or sincere about it at all. She just went on in that drawl of a monotone voice and said the same thing over again, "If he doesn't complete the test, he can't play." She knew full well these tests would not be given until the spring of the year and football season would be over by then. I left her office that day and so did any respect I might have had for her earlier. Michael never dealt with the downs of life very well. If things didn't work out as he thought they should have, he would immediately revert back to his self destructive behavior. That's just what he did. He started getting in more trouble. This time, he was arrested for having a cocaine like substance on his person and I forget what else. He was again, taken away from home. This time he was away for about a year. If I didn't lose my mind then, I think there's a good chance I'll remain sane until my death. I begin to refer to Michael as "my character builder" then for real, but just not so affectionately. He'd either make you or break you.

Cherylyn graduated from high school and I was beaming with pride at her graduation. She looked absolutely radiant as she marched in with her graduating class. After the ceremony, I let her hang out with her girlfriends for the night. She had always stuck right by my side and I thought she deserved a night out. She had practically raised her three younger brothers while I went to school and worked two, sometimes three jobs. We were always close even though we went through a trying period that most mothers and daughters go through I suppose. Still, we remained close. About two weeks after graduation, I was lying on my bed. Cherylyn came in and said, "Momma, I need to talk to you." I said, "Okay, what's up?" She said, "I'm pregnant." I'm glad I was already lying down or I'm sure I would have fallen on the floor. Tobias has mentioned about a month earlier that "Cherylyn looks pregnant Sweetheart; her Adam's apple looks swollen." Well, I had never ever heard of anyone detecting pregnancy by the size of their neck before and I always made sure I checked her soiled pads every month so I just blew Tobias off. Anyway, at that moment,I think I was more disappointed than angry. I said, "Cherylyn, you've worked hard to graduate just to have a baby and go through what I have with raising a child all by yourself?" She just sat on my bed and cried. Now, I thought to myself as I reflected back on graduation night, "I know why she looked so radiant."

Chapter 38

It was early summer. Doll called me and said, "Cheryl, you've never even been out of that small town. You've not seen any of the world and you've been through so much. You have been worried to death with Michael and you've never enjoyed any of your life. I don't want you to be like Mama and never do anything but sit and worry your life away. I'm going to take you on a dream vacation." That is exactly what she did. She told me to clear a week, put in for vacation from all of my jobs and ask Tyrone Jr. and Cherylyn to keep house and the children in my absence. So, that is what I did. Doll came to pick me up in a beautiful Lexus. I had never ridden in a luxury vehicle before. I drove for a while and it felt like I was riding on air. We arrived at her house in Georgia where I was immediately taken shopping by Doll. She bought me the most beautiful wardrobe of much needed clothes, shoes and accessories. Then she took me to the nail salon where I got a manicure and pedicure. I had never before had either and it was such a relaxing experience. I thoroughly enjoyed it. Then she and her husband Steve took me out to this fabulous restaurant where

I enjoyed the finest cuisine I had ever had. After sleeping like a bear in hibernation that night, the next morning, we were off to the airport. I had never flown anywhere before and I was a little apprehensive. Once seated, and in the air, I felt very relaxed. No one could tell me I wasn't Mrs. Rockerfeller. We landed in Montego Bay, Jamaica and what a beautiful place this was. The land was full of beautiful plants and flowers that seemed to have grown there naturally. The people and the environment were very colorful and lively. We rented a car and drove from Montego Bay to Ocho Rios. I drove to Ocho Rios and I enjoyed it very much. The steering wheel was on the right side of the car and, where we drove on the right side of the rode back home, here, one was to drive on the left side. Since I am left-handed, this was a piece of cake for me. When we reached the hotel, it was the most fabulous I had ever seen. The people all catered to us, something that I was certainly not accustomed to but was soon convinced that it wouldn't take long to become accustomed to it. The room was beautiful, the food and service exquisite. The Caribbean was beautiful and the water was just wonderful. It was crystal clear and comfortably warm. I could stand in it and see the very bottom of the sea. There were lots of daytime excursions that Doll booked for us and they all were great fun. We climbed Dunn's River Falls and shopped as the "liquid sunshine" gently fell to help hydrate our skin from the heat of the day. We shopped for hours at the different outdoor booths. As we island hopped from one place to another, we enjoyed the different kinds of foods and eating at the roadside outdoor cafes. We lounged at Irie Beach and rafted down the Martha Brae River. Life seemed really laid back here. It was as if the time of day really didn't matter. You didn't even need your watch if you didn't want to wear it. Ordering food was no different. If you were really hungry once you placed your order, you might be upset by the time the food arrived to your table. It took the chefs quite a while to prepare your order but once it arrived, it was well worth the wait. At night there seemed to be endless parties. I loved to see the natives dance. They had such a way of making dance lively. The ladies danced seductively and I remember thinking, "I must learn to dance like that so I can do that for Tobias once he's home." All in all, this idea of Doll's was a very enjoyable, very relaxing and a very much needed one. It was my very first real vacation and I love my sister for thinking of me and treating me like royalty for that entire week.

It has been said that "All good things must come to and end" and this was no different. I was soon back home with my family and back into the swing of running from one job to another again, all on minimal rest and sleep. I told the children of my wonderful vacation and they all wanted to go someday. I couldn't thank Doll enough and I told her how intrigued the children were with the pictures and my recollection of the trip. She promised that in the next couple of summers, she would send us all as a gift from her. On the weekend, I visited Tobias and told him all about the wonderful vacation that Doll had blessed me with. He was intrigued by my excitement and he just sat there and smiled at me as I rambled on and on. I told him that we must surely go there one day. He agreed.

Cherylyn had been sick and admitted to the hospital during my absence. Tyrone Jr. and his girlfriend had to really fill in for me. Cherylyn had hyperemesis gravidarium. She was throwing up everything she ate or drank and in the process, became dehydrated. She missed me I'm sure too. She was at home when I arrived though and she was just lying around looking miserable. She had a very low pain tolerance so I knew that she would definitely have to have an epidural once delivery was imminent, for her sake, mine, and the staff. We all went through the fall and winter with Cherylyn sitting under me at every available opportunity she got. She would not verbally say anything; instead, she would just nudge me and mouth the words, "I don't feel good." This really did get on my last nerves after nine full months of it but I remained patient. I would always tell her that she wasn't going to feel herself until after the baby was delivered.

I don't know what any of us would have done without my dear sister Doll because she was always so kind and thoughtful to all of us. About two weeks before the baby was to be born, Doll organized, from Georgia, a baby shower for Cherylyn. I've always enjoyed cooking and I made a spread fit for a king. AJ, as I nicknamed her, was not only a wonderful nurse and person; she was a wonderful cook as well. She made the most beautiful pink and blue baby bootie cake I have ever seen. It tasted as good as it looked too. Doll came up the day before the baby shower and with her she brought every size of baby clothing one would ever need. She had sizes that ranged from newborn to toddler. They were the most beautiful outfits I had ever seen. After the shower, Cherylyn did not need anything except for the baby to be born.

Finally, it was time for my very first grandchild to enter the world. I was assigned to work this particular night. Wanda, who was the charge nurse, assigned me to another patient. I thank her for that because as good of a nurse as I prided myself to be, I found, each time I checked on Cherylyn, I did not focus well as a nurse where she was concerned. To the staff's and my correct assumption, once the labor became intense, Cherylyn was not dealing with the pain very well at all. An epidural was placed and this relaxed her tremendously. When Cherylyn's cervix dilated to ten centimeters, it was time for her to start pushing. After about twenty minutes of pushing, my granddaughter was born. Cherylyn named her Raven Monae. Raven came out screaming bloody murder. She was such a beautiful baby. Tyrone Jr. was there with us the entire time and he just kept looking at her and asking me why she was crying so? I assured him that was what babies did when they were first born and that is exactly what we wanted her to do, cry. I explained to him that by crying, Raven was giving her lungs their very first exercise. As I was giving Raven her very first bath and shampoo, she continued to scream. Tyrone Jr. was allowed to watch as I bathed her. He wouldn't leave her side. Michael, who had come home from his latest trip to the juvenile center, John Lee and Malcolm came up to see their new niece as well. We all simply loved her. I had been very disappointed with Cherylyn for getting pregnant right at the time of her life when I had hoped she'd be focusing on going to college but Raven made everything all worthwhile. Thanks to Doll and my co-workers, when Raven and Cherylyn came home, Raven had everything that a baby could ever need. She cried most of the time, just like Cherylyn did when she was a baby. I was glad that Cherylyn had to deal with this crying day in and day out and not me.

True to Doll's promise, that summer, she financed a vacation for me, Cherylyn, Raven, Michael, John Lee, and Malcolm. Tyrone Jr. had to go to his two week drill in the National Guard so he wasn't able to go. His girlfriend, however, accompanied us. Fee, as we called her was a very hard-working, sweet young lady who had never seen much else than our small hometown as well, so I was glad that she was able to get another aspect of what life really held, as well as my own children. Doll sent us to Jamaica for an entire week, all expenses paid. Michael, who has always been a people person with a wonderful sense of humor, enjoyed the trip from start to finish. He kept the people that were seated near us on the plane in stitches with his endless shenanigans. Once we landed in Montego Bay, we rented a car and drove to Ocho Rios just as Doll and I had done the previous summer. We did a lot of island hopping and the children thoroughly enjoyed themselves. I enjoyed seeing them enjoy. We drove to Negril and visited the famous Rick's Café. There Michael and Chery-lyn were brave enough to jump off of the famous, more than 100 foot cliff and into the Caribbean. The children and Fee had a wonderful first vacation. This really did my heart good.

Chapter 39

It was a late fall night. I was working at the hospital. I received a telephone call from the police station. It had gotten to be that every time I saw a police car, my heart would seem to skip a beat. This time was no different. I was told to come down to the police station immediately. AJ, whom I had grown very close to, was my charge nurse on this night. She excused me and told me to go on down and see what was going on. When I arrived, there sat Michael in some Army fatigues. The police were holding him until I got there and I appreciated that of them. It seems that an off duty policeman saw Michael slumping behind a gas pump at a convenience store. He had a bag and inside the bag he had a fake pistol. It was assumed that he was going to try to rob this store. His "friends" as he termed them had talked him into doing this while they waited for him well out of harm's way. I was so frustrated with him until I just felt like screaming and never stopping. He was arrested and given probation this time and a home monitoring device on his ankle. I just wished that Michael would have chosen a positive set of friends and not have been a follower but a leader, but such was not the case. I thought, "Lord, I know I worried my mom almost to death running behind Tyrone Sr. but when will the harvest for those bad seeds I sowed end?" I was really at my wits ends. If God didn't help me to hold it together, I was certain that I would have a nervous breakdown. It was his younger brothers that kept me focused, through God's grace and mercy of course. I knew that I was all they had and if I lost it, they wouldn't have anyone.

Orlando seemed to rejoice over my child's downfall. He went around that small little town saying all kinds of derogatory, negative things about Michael. People of course seemed to love to bring back all the bad talk they heard. It would seem that Orlando would have tried to help me with Michael instead of glorying in our pain but he didn't. Then, his own personal pain started. He was living with this young girl who had four children of her own, three boys and a little girl. Dee was her name. She had gone out on the town one night and she said when she came back home a little earlier than expected, there she found Orlando groping her oldest son and having her son grope his private parts as well. She immediately called the police and Orlando was arrested. He had been sent to prison twice for robbing the same bank and I'm sure he knew that inmates labeled as child molesters didn't see much peace in prison. He was locked up in the county jail for an entire week. John Lee Jr. had come down to see about posting a bail for Orlando. It was about two days after Orlando was out of jail on bond when Evelyn called me. She sounded frantic on the telephone. She said, "Cheryl, Orlando is going to kill himself, I just know it because God has showed this to me." I said, "Evelyn, don't worry about that. I don't think he's going to kill himself. I'm here preparing a big meal for him now and John

Lee, Jr. is still here too. Orlando appears to be in good spirits." She insisted on speaking to him so I took the telephone outside where John Lee, Jr. and Orlando stood talking. I stood there listening as he reassured Evelyn that he was not about to do anything as foolish as harm himself. After about ten minutes of talking, they hung up. The very next day Evelyn called me again. She said, "Cheryl, I know he's going to do something to himself, I just can't shake this uneasy feeling I have." I again reassured her that he was indeed okay. I told her that I had been checking on him often and he seemed to be enjoying his two huge dogs that he loved so much and his fancy, brand new sports car he had just purchased.

It was a bright sunny summer Saturday. I, along with John Lee and Malcolm went to visit Orlando. It had been a week since he'd been home. All of my life, I have never felt comfortable being around Orlando for any length of time. He always had this explosive temper and would fight you for no reason at all. The level of comfort initially was no different on this day. The boys were going to the door and going in and out of it. Orlando and I were sitting in his living room on the sofa that had once been moms. The same sofa set that was a beautiful three piece ensemble that Evelyn had bought for mom and the same one Evelyn wanted me to have when mom died. Orlando had refused to give it to me and I certainly wasn't going to argue over it. His living room was very small and could not accommodate the love seat and coffee table. This tiny room was only large enough for the sofa and side chair so rather than give the love seat and coffee table to me; he chose to put it outside in the garage. Nonetheless, I loved him because he was my brother. Anyway, I scolded the boys for going in and out of the door because I just knew that it was only a matter of time before Orlando lost his cool. Instead, he just sat there on the sofa just as relaxed as I've ever seen him. He said, "Cheryl, leave them alone, they're not bothering anything." To say that I was shocked at his relaxed, laid back demeanor is putting it mildly. I had never seen my brother so thoroughly relaxed and mellowed out. I felt relaxed too with being around him on this day, for the very first time in my entire life. We sat there and I talked and talked almost incessantly as he sat there and listened patiently to my every word. I offered to fix him something to eat but he said he wasn't hungry. After about two hours of having the best visit I can ever remember having with him, I kissed him goodbye and we left.

About twelve mid night, I was awakened by this very loud pounding on the front door. I immediately got up to answer it. I don't know why I didn't think to turn on any lights but I didn't. I asked, "Who in the world is it?" The voice yelled back, "It's Bernie." I opened the door and there stood Bernie who was a dear friend of the family from way back. He had gone to school with John Lee, Jr. and Orlando and he used to come over to our house to visit with the family when I was a small child. He was now a police officer. I immediately asked him, "Is it my son or my brother?" He said, "Just let me come in." I opened the door and let him in and I asked, "Is it bad?" He appeared to be just as panicked as I was when he said, "It's bad, it's real bad." Still in the dark, I went over to the wicker set that I had in my living room and sat down. Bernie sat beside me. Then he went on. "It's your brother. He's dead. It appears that he took an overdose." I just sat there in silence groping his knee with what must have felt like a killer grip. I sat there speechless for so long until he finally broke the silence by asking me if he could use my phone. Without a word and still in total darkness, I got up and when I did, I started running. I ran to the back of the house where I couldn't run any further.

I then started screaming and all I could say was "Lord Jesus, Lord Jesus." All of this commotion had awakened Cherylyn and Michael. Cherylyn came to me and hugged me while asking, "Momma, what's wrong?" Each time I tried to talk, all that would come out of my mouth was "Lord Jesus!" Michael cut the light on and went into the living room where Bernie stood and asked him what was wrong. Bernie told him the horrible news.

After some time and I had regained some sort of composure, I called Tyrone Jr. He and Fee were at my house in what seemed like minutes. I managed to call Doll and Evelyn. Doll was hysterical on the telephone. Evelyn was very, very quiet. I couldn't believe any of this so I got Tyrone Jr. to ride down to the funeral parlor with me and there, it was confirmed that Orlando was indeed dead. I went to Mae's house and there I tried to console Orlando's son Marcus. I don't know who consoled whom because we each stood there in the middle of Mae's living room, holding each other and crying. When John Lee, Jr. arrived, I found out the real story. Orlando had not taken any pills. Bernie told John Lee, Jr. that he just told me that because he didn't want to tell me just how gruesome it really was. As it turned out, Orlando had recorded messages for John Lee, Jr., David, and Evelyn. He told them that he had lived a good life and not to worry about him, he would be just fine. Then he had drank some liquor, smoked some cigarettes, then called Dee to inform her that he was about to kill himself. Afterward, he took one of the pillows that went with mom's beautiful living room set, placed it on one side of his head, put a gun on the other side of his head and pulled the trigger. I have never heard David curse but this time, David was very upset. He said, "Now this time, at least I know he can't do any more stupid shit." I didn't know exactly but his statement made me wonder if Orlando had tried to molest David as a child. Even though he was my brother, his death somehow brought with it a sense of relief for me as well. When I was four years old, Orlando would call me upstairs in his room. Being afraid of him, I would go to see what he wanted. Once I was inside the room where it was very dim, he would pull my panties down and stick his finger inside of me. I was afraid of him so I didn't know what to do. After he did this, he would give me a fifty cent coin and threaten me that he would kill me if I told mom. This happened three times. After the third time, I saw blood in my panties and I told mom what had been happening and showed her my panties. I don't know what was done about it because mom nor dad ever said anything about it. I just know that he never touched me again as a young child.

The next incident I remember was when I was 26 years old. Every year, mom and dad would go to North Carolina to their church convocation for a week. Each year, I used this time to give their house a thorough cleaning. This particular day I had finished cleaning their house and was in the shower. I had locked all the doors but I heard someone in the house. I became alarmed. Then someone was at the bathroom door. Somehow Orlando had gotten the bathroom door opened and came in with me standing there stark naked and dripping wet. He tried to rape me but I fought him tooth and nail. I had never fought that hard in my entire life. Then, just as suddenly as he entered the bathroom, he ran out of the bathroom and out of the house. I was terribly shaken. I immediately called mom and dad in North Carolina. When they came home, they never mentioned another word about that either. Anyway, I was now relieved that I wouldn't have to worry about any other occurrences from him ever again. I was very sad though that he had taken his own life. I felt bad that he was that sad and unhappy of a person. I loved him because he was my brother. It had been three years since the death of my parents when this unfortunate thing took place. I'm just thankful that mom and dad weren't around to see this. If mom hadn't already been dead, I'm almost certain this would have killed her. We buried him right next to mom and dad.

Chapter 40

Through the years, Martha and I had grown apart. I didn't feel close to her because I would later find out that she allowed Tyrone Sr. to bring his women to her house. Martha knew about the children he had fathered as well but she always stood up for him, right or wrong. When I learned about this, it caused me to lose a lot of respect for her. Anyway, she had been sick and started going to the hospital for frequent admissions. I decided to let by gones be by gones. I would let Cherylyn use my new car that the Lord had blessed me with to take her on any errands she needed to go on. Their spending time together made them grow close as well. The last time Martha went into the hospital, she died. The children were very hurt by her death. We had just buried Orlando and now another sad occasion to go through. When would this madness end is all I could think.

When we entered the chapel, there lay Martha. She looked very nice and her casket was also very nice. Queeta had done an excellent job making the arrangements. I'm sure Queeta had to make all of the arrangements by herself because Tyrone

Sr. could never be counted on to help with much of anything. Michael took Martha's death very hard. At her funeral, he just sat there in front of me and looked at her coffin as the tears streamed down his face. I felt helpless because I didn't know what to do to console him. After the funeral, we all went back to the church where dinner was served. Tyrone Sr. found his way over to where the children and I were seated. Terry was sitting with us as well. I had taken him to be one of my sons. He looked just like my sons too. He and Tyrone Jr. could easily have passed for twins. He loved to hang around me and the children and he would spend the night with us often. Whenever he would come to visit, I would go out of my way to prepare foods that I knew Terry loved. He was a very comical guy and he said, "Oh well, the ace of spades finally hit the deck" referring to Martha's love for a card game. That broke the monotony. Then Tyrone Sr. started talking with that proper, foreign, fake accent that he had used so many times before on our shopping adventures. I just sat there eating my food and tried to ignore him. Then he said, "I have seventeen children." After he said that all I could think was, "You sorry dog. You have the nerve to say you have seventeen children and I'd bet my eye tooth that you haven't helped to take care of a single one of them." I kept my cool though because this was not the time or the place to start any mess. After this whole thing was over, I felt relieved. Before the children and I left, Tyrone Sr. came over to me and hugged me and whispered in my ear, "Thank you for taking good care of my children." What I should have done was smack his face. Instead, I just walked away.

Chapter 41

Ithank God for giving Tobias to me because his presence in my life kept me grounded. Even on my worst feeling day, each time he called or I visited him, I hung up or left with a renewed vitality and outlook on life. Even though he could not physically be with me to help me during Michael's dilemmas, help me financially or with any of the recent drama that I had to go through, his presence could be sensed even when he wasn't physically around me and that feeling always brought a smile to my face and comfort to my heart strings. He still knew how to make me blush like a teenager. He always sent me the most heartfelt cards and letters and this made my day as well. It was our anniversary again and I received a beautiful card from him. He had a real talent for writing and this card was just what the doctor ordered. He wrote:

Today is more than an Anniversary to me. It's more than just Valentine's Day where it is anticipated that something special be done in the name of love for that significant other in our lives. This day is more than you can imagine beloved because I love you far deeper than one holiday or milestone in our lives could ever indicate.

For six years and counting you've been the focal point that motivates me to rise above circumstances and obstacles. To just say "thank you" is not enough; Celebrating and/or demonstrating my love for you on this day each year is inadequate.

In light of this, I am faced with the challenge of how best to arrange words, phrases, and sentences that convey to you the absolute inviolability of the love I have for you. It only takes the following 19 words:

I love you immeasurably, affectionately, passionately, absolutely, and I intend to do so for the rest of my life.

We went through the spring quite uneventfully. Michael was in the eighth grade and doing pretty well. He was managing to stay out of trouble. John Lee was in the sixth grade and doing very well too. John Lee's shortcoming with me was that he was always very sassy and fussy. I sure gave him the right name everyone agreed. He could always make me go there out of all of my children. He always had to have the last word. Malcolm was now in kindergarten. He had a great first year in pre-kindergarten and he excelled in everything that the teacher gave him to learn. He was anxious to learn everything there was to learn it seemed. Cherylyn had adjusted quite nicely to being a mom though she had already had years of experience with her little brothers. She had moved out and into her own apartment and she was enjoying her newfound freedom. All in all, I was content. At the end of the summer, the children went back to school.

It was Thanksgiving eve. Tyrone, Jr. had come by the

house earlier to get some money to make some pecan pies for Thanksgiving dinner. After cooking a few items, I laid down in preparation to go to work at seven that evening. When I arrived at work, AJ had made some very tasty foods. She loved to cook and she sure was a great cook, "almost as good as me", I smiled to myself. I was having a pretty good time at work. We were usually very busy but that night we were able to have some down time. About two o'clock am, Tyrone Jr. called me. He was talking so fast I could hardly understand what he was saying. I asked him to slow down and when he did, he began to tell me that he had been arrested but he was okay. I asked him what on earth he had been arrested for. He just said, "Momma, everything is okay so don't worry about me please." After he hung up, I just sat there dumbfounded holding the telephone. I had never had any trouble from Tyrone Jr. and now here he was telling me that he had been arrested. He had never been in trouble in his life. I called Fee and asked her what was going on but she didn't seem to know much except that he had borrowed her car for the evening. I stayed at work and it was a blessing that we weren't busy that night. I just sat and stared at nothing. I can't even express on paper just how I felt. Perhaps I'm not even sure myself. The next morning at shift change, Vee came in to work. I was crying when I told her what had happened to Tyrone Jr. I found out that he had been charged with robbing some people and taking menial things all totaling $350.00. I knew that he had to have been drunk or on something that night because I knew my son. He had never given me any trouble. He had always been my right hand man. He never talked back to me, he was a good son. My heart was truly broken. Vee just stood there and hugged me and cried with me. She loved Tyrone Jr. too. She always teased him whenever she saw him. He loved her as well.

I called in for the next day because I just didn't have the energy, physically, mentally, emotionally, spiritually, nothing. The supervisor tried to give me a hassle at first but I told her that my son had been arrested and I just wasn't feeling it. Then she understood. Cherylyn and her friend Dan Lee had moved into Dad's house. Dan Lee and Tyrone Jr. were very good buddies. Dan Lee was a very nice guy. I liked him for Cherylyn. He was good with Raven too. They both went to drill together and were battle buddies I think. We had Thanksgiving Dinner over at their house and I don't know how any of us managed to get through it, but we did. The food was very good. Dan Lee and Cherylyn did a great job. No one seemed to have much of an appetite though. Dan Lee seemed very nervous and sad but I attributed that to the recent events.

Early the next morning, Cherylyn called me. She said "Momma, the police have come and picked up Dan Lee." I was totally shocked. I asked her what happened. She said, "It has something to do with Tyrone Jr. I think." Well, as it turned out, he was accused of being with Tyrone Jr. on this crazy, very unnecessary night of events. This all was too much for me to deal with. First I'd lost the most important person in my life, mom. Then I'd lost dad nine months later. Then Orlando goes and does a selfish thing as taking his own life, not thinking enough about the loved ones he would leave behind-his son, grown into the very fine man that he had become, his grandsons, granddaughters, us. Michael constantly in and out of trouble over some stupid, unnecessary stuff, now Tyrone Jr. in a world of trouble over nothing!! Not to mention the small town full of a lot of nosey, narrow minded people that obviously had no business of their own. Doll would later give me a saying that I wish I had back then. It goes, "the best business in any line of business is to have some business of your own. But if you have no business, then make it your business, to leave other people's business alone." Whoever said those words, I agree with wholeheartedly. I'd had it with the whole thing.

Doll had continuously asked me to move to Georgia. There didn't seem to be a more perfect time than the present. This town, I thought, had nothing for the young children or anyone else for that matter to do but to get into trouble. There was no movie theatre, no skating rink, no bowling alley, no entertainment at all except eating and clubbing. The nearest movie, skating or bowling establishments was either 19 miles south or 42 miles north. A lot of the people that I knew didn't even have transportation. This, I now felt, was the perfect setting for my sons to get nowhere fast, except for in trouble. I just couldn't see any growth for us here. So many painful memories were here as well. I decided I would move as soon as the children finished the school year. The humungous drawback I had with this decision was leaving Tobias and not being able to spend every weekend and holiday with him as I had always done for the past six years. I never missed a visiting day unless there just was no visiting allowed for whatever reason. I didn't want to leave Tyrone Jr. alone at this time in his life either but I felt my sanity and my children's very welfare was now on the line.

That weekend, when I visited Tobias, I told him that I needed to move away. I told him that I loved him and I'd always love him but I just had to do this. I tried to explain this to him so that he could feel what I was feeling. I know that he didn't want me to move away but Tobias has never been the type to demand that I did or did not do something, whether he was opposed to it or not. He just sat there quietly listening to me. Then, after some time he said, "Cheryl, do we need to get a divorce before you leave?" I thought that was a very odd question but knowing Tobias like I had come to know him, he always had a deeper reason for his questions. I assured him that we would not need a divorce and that I would continue to be faithful to him and in love with him, even with the distance between us. I knew that he would not be getting frequent, or probably any visits now because in the seven years that I'd known him, his family still did not visit him. His mother visited about two times but that was all. His father never visited and none of them, including his parents, sister or brothers wrote to him. I felt bad that I would not be there to visit him or Tyrone Jr., but quite honestly, I was fed up with running from the jail to the prison environment and I was ready for a change of pace. I needed a change, probably more mental than anything else. I needed a fresh start and I felt there was no time like the present.

The home that I had prayed and worked so hard for now had no significance to me whatsoever. I knew that if I didn't pay the mortgage, the home would surely go into foreclosure, yet, none of that mattered to me now. I decided to move into my childhood home with Cherylyn and Raven until the school year ended. I figured this way; I would be able to save money. So, early January, we all moved to mom and dad's house. As it turned out, Cherylyn became very ill and had to go into the hospital to have surgery. She was unable to work so my presence in dad's home became a blessing for her and Raven as well. I wasn't able to save as much money as I had hoped too though because I had to pick up the slack for Cherylyn and Raven. I continued to work the two jobs, all on very little sleep. John Lee and Malcolm continued to do excellent in school. Michael had gotten into more trouble and was once again, in the hands of the police. He was again placed in a

juvenile detention center. I was more determined to get out of
town now more than ever because I actually thought I would
loose what mind I had left if I didn't.

In March during spring break, the two boys and I drove
to Georgia. We stayed for the week and during that week I
submitted my resume to several nursing agencies and hospitals. I also sent the necessary paperwork to the State Board
Nursing Office so that I could obtain a nursing license for that
state. I then went looking for apartments. I had never lived in
an apartment before but I was determined to make this much
needed change. I found a very nice apartment and left a deposit on it. My week had proven very fruitful indeed. Doll was
very pleased that I was finally leaving and moving close to
her but she said she still would not believe it until she actually
saw me there with my children and all of my belongings. At
the end of the week, I drove back to Virginia with a wonderful
feeling of self accomplishment.

Chapter 42

The end of the school year was rapidly approaching. I had submitted my two weeks resignation. I really don't think many people took my idea of moving away seriously because I had never left my small home town for any real length of time before. Anyway, I reserved a U-Haul and began packing all of my lifelong belongings. John Lee was sad because he didn't want to leave his friends but I assured him that he would meet new friends. Malcolm was probably too young to worry much about it because he didn't seem to mind one way or another. I asked Cherylyn to come with us because she had never been away from her family and there was no real family left except Tobias and Tyrone Jr. She didn't want to leave though.

It seemed that every night at work, I was given a going away party. The girls in OB felt more like my sisters than my co-workers and I knew I would miss them terribly. At last, it was the weekend I was to leave the state. I went to see Tobias and we had a very nice visit. I thank him now for making my decision to leave as stress free as possible. I knew that it hurt him to see me and the children leave because it hurt me to leave him, but he never once said one negative word about it. After visiting him, I went to see Tyrone Jr. I assured him that I would come back for his trial and I would come back to see him as frequently as I could. I did not go to see Michael before I left. To tell the truth, I was very disappointed in Michael. I had hoped that he would be moving with us and I couldn't make any sense of the things he did to wind up in trouble. His getting into trouble worried me too much and brought my spirits way down. I didn't need my spirits down now. I was going to great lengths to make a fresh start. I knew that when I came back to visit, I wouldn't think of leaving without seeing him though. I loved him so much. If only he would learn to love himself. I wish I could have made him see that Tyrone Sr. not only left him, he left us all. Somehow, I prayed he would get past that pain and anger. It was only hurting him and us. Tyrone Sr. couldn't feel one bit of Michael's pain and probably couldn't have cared less anyway.

On the day before I was to leave, I went to the U-Haul company only to find that there had been a mistake made in my truck reservation. The only large truck that was left was this huge, huge truck that was very loud. The man explained to me that there was a leak in the exhaust system. That, he said, was why the truck was so loud. I just knew I would be deaf by the time I reached my 500+ mile destination. Nonetheless, I managed to drive it to mom's house and the children and I loaded all of our belongings into it. I had a hitch for my car and we managed to hook that up too. That next morning, the boys and I kissed Cherylyn and Raven goodbye and we started out on our journey. My dear cousin Lisa and her two children decided to drive down with me to help us get settled in so they followed close behind in her car. I felt just like a rhinestone cowgirl driving down the interstate in that huge, loud rig with a hitch attached to the back of it that carried my car.

Even though it was a very tiresome, very loud trip, we arrived in about eight hours. We went to Doll's house where she had a delicious spaghetti dinner waiting for us all. My apartment was not scheduled for our occupancy until the next day, Monday, so we spent the night at Doll's house as well. I'm sure I snored to high heaven because I was just that exhausted.

Early the next morning, we drove to the apartment complex and I paid the rest of the money which was the 1st month's rent. When we got to the apartment, we all were very pleased. It was only two bedrooms but it was very spacious and I really didn't need a huge place. After all, it was only me and the two boys. Lisa and her children were a big help in getting us all unpacked and settled in. My nursing license had not been issued for Georgia yet and I was somewhat concerned about that. I wasn't able to save as much as I had hoped to because of Cherylyn's illness and surgery so, as much as I tried not to worry, I did. I knew God would provide for us because He had on numerous occasions before, but I still found myself worrying about my license.

It had been a month and still, no license. I had to pay the rent and I needed groceries for my boys and me. I told Doll about this and she and her husband Steve came over and gave me five one hundred dollar bills. I couldn't thank them enough. After they left, I went inside my bedroom and got down on my knees and cried out to the Lord. I just couldn't thank Him enough for all of His many blessings. The parable that Dad had given me so long ago about the wind and the leaves came rushing back and then, a sense of relaxation overtook me. I knew that somehow, everything was going to be alright. I still didn't get my license until the next month but God had blessed me to work with this nursing agency. They accepted my Virginia license and were able to go online to verify that I didn't have any restrictions on my license and that I had applied for my Georgia license. That job was a real blessing let me tell you. It paid the rent and the bills and fed me and my boys.

That August, I registered the boys in school. School was very different from back home. John Lee was in the eighth grade and since his new school was more than a mile from the apartment, he rode the bus to his school. Because Malcolm's school was less than a mile from our apartment, he had to walk to school. Let me tell you that I was very uncomfortable letting him walk to and from school in a big city and him being only six years old. He had been used to me taking him and picking him up from school back home. As it turned out, I was worried over nothing. Malcolm soon found little friends that lived in the same apartment complex and though I carried him to school in the mornings, he would walk back with them in the afternoons. He was becoming a real little man. He continued to excel in school and I was very proud of him and John Lee. I was happy that John Lee was adapting to his new environment especially after he was so heartbroken about leaving his friends. He quickly made new friends and they were good friends as well.

It was the night before my birthday. I had tucked the boys in to bed and decided to chill out and enjoy the quiet time. I had bought an adult movie and I had a joint of weed. I thought I owed it to myself to celebrate. I wished Tobias could be with me but since he could not be, I decided to smoke the weed and hopefully, I would be carefree, for a little while anyway. I was sitting in dad's recliner, the same one that I had placed in my living room for him to enjoy only a few years ago. I had on my nightgown and I was watching television. I had not put the movie in yet nor had I lit the joint. All of a sudden, I turned my head away from the television and looked to my left side. I found myself pleading with this invisible presence. I was saying, "But God, I'm not ready to die. I want to live to raise my children to see them grown and able to take care of themselves." Then in another breath I said, "But God, I'm not ready to die. I'm not saved and I don't want to go to hell." Well, I certainly was not high because I hadn't even lit the joint and I couldn't figure out why I was saying these things. No less than two minutes after my pleading with God not to take my life, John Lee came running up the hallway. He was frantic as he said, "Oh momma, thank God you're not dead! I just had a bad dream! I dreamed you were dead and you were sitting right here in this chair with that nightgown on!" To say that I was horrified would be putting it mildly. I was scared out of my wits. I don't know who was more shaken, John Lee or me. Needless to say, I didn't smoke the joint nor put in the adult movie. I went to my bedroom and got on my knees and thanked God for sparing my life. Then I asked John Lee if he would sleep in my bed with me that night and he did. Long after John Lee had fallen back to sleep, I lay awake in bed with my heart beating so loud it seemed that I could hear it without a stethoscope. I don't think I went to sleep that night. I was too afraid.

Chapter 43

In the fall of the year, I was blessed with a job that had benefits. I had remained hypertensive after Malcolm's birth but I had been going without my blood pressure medicine because I did not have any health insurance. Now, finally I could get to see a doctor and get my medicine. I had worked a lot of night shifts for the agency and I'm thankful that my blood pressure rarely got dangerously high during that period of not having the medicine to take. Although I was thankful for my new job, I hated the hours. I went to work at one o'clock in the evening and got home after twelve midnight. Those hours were not conducive to having the sole responsibility of a soon to be teenager and a six year old. I asked my supervisor if I could change shifts because I explained to her that I was a single parent and I really needed to be home during those crucial hours. She listened to me intently and said she understood but said that my present hours were the only available hours. I knew those hours were not good for us but I really didn't have a choice so I stayed there.

It was late October. I received a telephone call from my old hospital in Virginia and immediately, my heart started thumping in my chest. It was Queeta. She was going on and on about Cherylyn having a stroke and Raven was with them and I had to come to get Raven. I couldn't make any sense of any of this. I felt that Cherylyn was much too young to have had a stroke. So, here I was, just starting a new job and having to ask the supervisor for time off already. She was very sweet about it and granted me excused leave. Evelyn lived in Alabama which was less than a two hour drive from us. I called her and told her what was going on and she agreed to come to pick John Lee and Malcolm up and carry them back home with her. I knew that the boys would be in excellent hands with Evelyn and I was so very thankful for that. I was also thankful that it was the weekend and they wouldn't have to miss any school. So, after seeing the boys off, I set out for the long drive back to Virginia. When I reached the hospital, I found that Cherylyn had been taken to a hospital in Richmond so, after picking up Raven, I continued the two hour drive to check on Cherylyn. When I arrived at the hospital the nurses would not answer any of my questions but instead directed me to her room. She was sitting there on the bed quietly. When I spoke to her, I noticed that her speech was indeed slurred. She wanted me to check her out of the hospital and that is what I did. She said she wanted to come back to Georgia with me and I figured it would be less trouble to check on her and Raven if they were near me so I complied. I noticed that as Cherylyn walked, she dragged one of her feet and I was concerned about that.

Once we arrived back to our hometown, we had to stay at my old house. Although it was in the process of being foreclosed upon, I had allowed Cherylyn and Raven to live there. Sometime during the summer, David and his wife had come down and ordered Cherylyn to pay rent for staying at mom and dad's house or move out. I heard that was a really bad scene and in the end, Cherylyn had to move. We spent the night at my old house and early the next morning, after packing their meager belongings, we started the long journey back to Georgia. When we arrived, I made her and Raven comfortable in our, now seemingly very small, apartment. I prepared food for them and I noticed that although Cherylyn's speech was slurred and she dragged her left foot when she walked while supporting her left arm with her right one, her appetite was not at all affected. She ate everything I prepared for her and then some. I soon began to question whether or not she had made this whole thing up.

It turned out that she had indeed made this all up. I told her that she really didn't have to go to these extremes to get down here with us. After all, I had asked her to move with me from the very beginning. As time passed, Cherylyn and I quarreled a lot. I felt imposed upon. She was not working and I again, had the responsibility of taking care of her and Raven. I had made this drastic life change to make things better for me and the boys and to have some peace of mind. Now it seemed that the same problems and issues had followed me. Where Cherylyn and I had always been very close, we now started to grow apart, quickly.

It was Christmastime. John Lee always loved this time of year. He always decorated the house so this year was no different. He loved to decorate the tree and could do a great job with it. After he finished his elaborate decorating, if you weren't in the Christmas spirit beforehand, you certainly were in it afterward, looking around the place. Cherylyn was working some now at a grocery store. I had given her a deadline to have her own place so she was trying to adhere to that. She had never been very good at being able to provide for herself and Raven but I didn't feel like continuing to be the sole provider for everyone either. I managed to get through the holidays and even though I missed Tobias all of the time, holidays seemed to be much worse with me. Still, I would try to go through the motions of having a wonderful time for the boys' benefit.

The New Year arrived uneventfully and with it came news of the trial for Tyrone Jr. I was determined to be there for him as I had promised. News also arrived that it was time for me to pick Michael up from the juvenile detention center as well. It's funny how both these dates coincided with the other but it really was convenient for me as well. I had decided to resign from my job, largely due to the inconvenient hours and I had just been blessed with a terrific job that I loved. The hours were a dream come true, more like a prayer that was answered. The hours were from 8:30 am to 5:00 pm and I had every weekend and holiday off. It was just perfect for me and the boys. I could see John Lee off on the bus and could continue to carry Malcolm to school. Even though he continued to walk home in the afternoons, it wouldn't be long before I would be home with the both of them. I could monitor homework and their other activities as well. This job was really a big blessing.

So, here I was again in a position where I had to ask for time off from work just after starting a new job. I went to my new nursing supervisor. Mrs. James was her name and what a nice, understanding person she was. Before now, I had not felt comfortable talking about all of the troubles I was going through with anyone, but she was different. I felt very comfortable with her. Whenever I was really feeling down and depressed, Mrs. James would send me an email or come by the office where I was working to give me something to read that she had printed or purchased. God really used her to uplift my sinking spirits and to let me know that He had not forgotten me, even in the midst of my trials. I thank God for her to this day. I told her about my situation and she granted me the time that I needed. It was a blessing for Cherylyn to still be living with us at the time because I left the boys in her care as I drove, all night, down that long highway home once again. Thankfully, my old house was still vacant and my key still fit the lock. My money was very limited and I had a blow out as soon as I arrived back home so being able to stay in my old house was a blessing. Later that morning after lying down for a while, I drove the car to the tire shop. I left it there for repairs as I walked to the courthouse, my heart sinking with every step that I took. I was so tired of going to a courthouse, being involved with the court system and everything that was associated with it, yet I kept stepping right along. Once inside, I sat there and just watched as so many young Black men sat there waiting to go before the judge and I was deeply saddened. Then Tyrone Jr. was brought in. He was handcuffed and had shackles on his ankles as well. My first thought was to start screaming as loud as I could but that wouldn't have helped anything. I probably would have gotten thrown out of the courtroom and taken to the mental ward at the hospital. Instead, I just sat there and started praying. I was asked to come up and testify on his behalf. I had already prayed and asked God to give me every word to say so surprisingly, I wasn't afraid. The prosecutor for the state was none other than Ms. Pearson, the very same person that had, just a few years before, represented Tobias in his trial. Anyway, when I spoke, I could only say the truth. I said that I had never had any problems with Tyrone Jr. growing up. He had been my right hand, helping me with his sister and brothers. He graduated at the age of sixteen and went directly into the Army. After completing his AIT training as a medic, he worked full time and was in the National Guard. I said that he had never been in trouble with the law before; this was his first time. I begged the judge to take this into consideration before imposing sentencing on him. The state of Virginia had passed a no parole law four years earlier so I knew that all of the people who had come into the system in the past four years would have to serve 85% of their sentence. After I stepped down, Ms. Pearson began to speak. I really don't know what all she said because it was as if my brain went numb. Anyway, at the conclusion of his trial, I heard the judge sentence my son to 14 years. I immediately jumped up and headed for the door when I hear a voice calling me. I stopped and when I turned around, it was Ms. Pearson. She asked, "Cheryl, can I speak with you for minute?" I honestly was not in a "speaking to" mood but through my tears, I said yes. She led me into this little room outside of the courtroom and she said, "I know you hate me, I know you hate me. He didn't keep his promise to me so I had to prosecute him to the fullest extent of the law." All I could say was, "I don't hate you, I don't hate anyone." I then left and started walking back down the street to the repair shop. I was so grief stricken. I felt at that moment that death would have been a welcome thing for me.

When I arrived at the shop, I was told that I had done some more damage when I continued to drive the car after the blow out. The repairs would cost more than I had at the time. I had enough money for food for Michael and me and for gas to get back home with, not very much else. I made an arrangement with the owner to pay him as soon as I got back to Georgia and worked a shift at the agency. He was nice enough to let me. As soon as that business was concluded, on I drove to the outskirts of Richmond to pick Michael up. My whole body felt numb. I think that was my defense mechanism now looking back on it. If I had not gone numb, I fear that I would have gone completely insane. There is truly a thin line between sanity and insanity and I felt I was dangerously bordering it. I picked Michael up without incidence and after stopping to pick up food, we drove back to the house that I had once been so proud to call home. I told Michael that we would be leaving for Georgia in the morning but it was imperative that I visit Tyrone Jr. that night. So that night, I drove to the jail to check on Tyrone Jr. and I thank God that I did. Michael did not have ID so he had to wait outside for me.

When I went into the visiting area, there sat Tyrone Jr. He had been made a trustee at the jail almost as soon as he was locked up so he was already out of his cell and waiting for me as I entered. We just sat there looking through the glass at each other. Then, suddenly Tyrone Jr. started talking very fast. He said, "Momma, don't worry about me, I'm going to be just fine." Before I could say anything he went on. He said, "I've got it all figured out. I'm going to be down there with you and Aunt Doll soon. I already know what I'm going to do." Well, with these words, my heart sank even further, as if it could. I pleaded with him now, "Please Tyrone, you've already let the devil fool you into this trouble, please, please don't try to escape or do anything foolish. If you try to escape, they're going to shoot you and they're going to shoot to kill." Then I broke down. I couldn't handle it any longer. I just started sobbing as I called on the Lord right then and there. Through my sobs, all I could manage to say was "Lord Jesus, Lord Jesus" over and over again. Then Tyrone Jr. said, "Momma, do you know how long it took me to get to be 14 years old!" Right after he asked me that question, he got up and walked as far as he could go to the end of the room he was in. He just stood there leaning against the wall with his back to me. I knew he was sobbing as well.

As I walked out of the jail and headed for the parking lot, there stood Michael waiting for me. I'm so glad he was standing there because as soon as I approached him, my legs buckled and if he had not grabbed me and held onto me, I surely would have fallen on the cement. My legs just didn't seem to work and I couldn't stop crying. Michael was there for me that night and I thank God for that. He hugged me and helped me to walk to the car, all the while soothing me and telling me not to cry. Now I can see why his release date and Tyrone's court date were on the same day. God knew I would need some support and he had placed Michael just where and when I needed him.

Chapter 44

Once we arrived in Georgia, I had to take Michael to the juvenile probation office to get him established there. Then I took him to the nearby high school to get him enrolled. We immediately ran into trouble. I was not familiar with Georgia's laws so I was totally shocked when I was told that because Michael's school records indicated he had been in a detention center, he would have to go to alternative school. I didn't even know what an alternative school was. Michael was very upset and disappointed as well. He had high hopes of coming to Georgia, getting in school and getting back to playing sports. There were no sports offered in the alternative school. I missed more time from work as I fought to appeal this decision not to let Michael attend regular public school, all to no avail. Once I had done everything I knew to do and had failed, I explained to Michael that he would have to go to this school for a while, at least until he could prove himself to the school board. Well, as I said before, Michael never handled disappointment very well and this time was no different. When I would see John Lee and Malcolm off to school, I would then take Michael to the alternative school since there wasn't any school bus service for it. As soon as Michael would get there, he would leave. I think he might have gone to this school a week if that long. I had gone to great lengths to make a fresh start and it seemed that all the drama I was running away from had followed me right down the road.

One evening when I arrived home, I was confronted by the apartment manager. She told me that Malcolm and one of his little friends had been playing outside and one of them started a grass fire. She said because this was a real hazard, I would have to move. Because Malcolm didn't actually start the fire, she gave me a month before I had to vacate the apartment. The other little boy's family had to leave immediately. I didn't know what to think or do at first. I was really disappointed that John Lee or Michael couldn't have supervised things any better than they did, at least until I got home in the evenings. This dream of a fresh start was beginning to turn into a nightmare. Cherylyn and Raven had moved out because the apartment was too small for all of us. It was never meant to accommodate anyone but me and the boys in the first place. Now I was faced with having to relocate. I really didn't know the area that well so Cherylyn told me about these apartments that were "very nice." I was desperate and pressed for time so I went to check them out. They seemed okay so I put my deposit down and in thirty days, we would be ready to go. On the day we were moving, Michael and another guy Cherylyn had met named Carl was over helping us. After we loaded the U-Haul, I walked to the car to put a few more things in the trunk. It was then that I noticed the right front tire. It was totally bent. I panicked. I asked "What on earth happened to my car?" When I got in and started it up, the oil light was on and oil was pouring from the car and onto the ground. In the short time that I was in the house making sure we hadn't forgotten anything, Michael had taken my car and gone somewhere and totally messed it up. Then he brought it back and parked it as if nothing had happened. I was furious! I drove the car to a shop where I left it for repairs. I had to use the U-Haul truck to move with, do grocery shopping with and everything else that day. Michael continued to deny it and that made me even angrier because I knew he had ruined my car. I just didn't know why. I had to take public transportation to work until my car was repaired. When I was able to get the car out of the shop, it never was repaired properly. It continued to leak oil as well. I was too through with Michael.

This new apartment was not in Malcolm's school district so I had to put him in day care. This was another extra, unnecessary bill for me. I didn't want to change his school right there in the middle of the second semester so this was my only other alternative. Cherylyn had moved in the same apartment complex with me. We still were not getting along very well and this made me sad. We had always been the best of friends when she was growing up and now it seemed as if she was my enemy or something. She was my only daughter for Pete's sake! Anyway, this move and this apartment complex turned out to be not such a good move. The apartments had a lot of undesirable characters in it and wouldn't you know Michael would befriend them? He wasn't going to school and it seemed that I couldn't make him. When I told the probation officer he wasn't going to school, he placed him in a school there in the probation building but Michael wasn't doing much of anything there either. Cherylyn was coming over to my house when I was at work doing her laundry and taking food from my house. I had told her not to come over when I was not home but she paid this not one bit of attention.

One day I came home from work and Cherylyn was there doing her laundry, again. Doll and her daughter were there as well as Michael, John Lee and Malcolm. When I came inside and saw Cherylyn doing her laundry after I had asked her not to come over if I wasn't home and not to do her laundry over at my house, I became angry. I told her to leave right then and I opened the front door and gave her a shove. Well, why did I do that? She started fighting me in my own home. When she hit me, as I went to hit her, Michael grabbed me and held me. In the process of him holding me, Cherylyn proceeded to punch me. She punched me in my face and right in my eye. I had never before in my life had a black eye but I sure did now. After cursing me out even worse than she probably would have cursed a total stranger, while telling me she didn't have "no mother" she left. I grabbed my niece and hugged her tightly while I cried as my niece just stood there rubbing my back. After this incident, I found it impossible to be around her for a long while. I didn't feel like she had a mother either. I warned Michael that if he ever, again in his life, held me while someone beat on me, when I did get loose, I would kill him. I meant it. I later told Cherylyn that if she ever put as much as a finger on me ever again, one of us would be going to jail and the other would be going to the morgue. I meant it.

Chapter 45

I was very lonesome indeed. I was feeling very sorry for myself. I felt I needed companionship. This is when I started having an affair. I met this guy where I worked and we started talking. It was refreshing to have someone of the opposite sex to have an adult conversation with and just to spend time with period. Where I was writing Tobias on a regular basis, it now became sporadic. When he called, I didn't want to talk to him. I think it was because I was feeling so guilty. I knew he knew something was going on with me but he wasn't sure. So, for about six months, I did not write him or keep him abreast of the things that were going on with us as I had always done. During the entire time of my emotional absence from Tobias, he never stopped writing me and attempting to reach out to me. I really felt that I was tired of waiting for him. He had been denied parole twice now and I was beginning to feel like he would not be coming home anytime soon and that he would indeed "do everyday of his time" as Mr. McKine had boldly stated earlier. With Tobias continuing to reach out to me and pour his soul out to me and continue to love me despite my lack of returning his affection as I had always done before, I started to feel very guilty. Then I began to take a good look at this guy and I started asking myself, "Is he really worth you losing your husband over? Do you think he could love you as your husband does? Do you think you could love him to the same degree that you love your husband? Will this man love your children like Tobias does?" The answers to all of these questions were no. The children didn't like the guy anyway, especially Malcolm. Malcolm stayed angry all of the time it seemed. He would walk around the house with his fists clenched. He continued to make all A's in school but he was a very angry little boy. Malcolm loved his dad with all of his heart. He had never seen his dad mistreat me in any way and he certainly was mad at me right now. I decided that this guy was nowhere near worth losing my husband over or the respect of my children. So, as quickly as this foolish, meaningless affair started, it ended.

I was now faced with not knowing whether to be totally honest with Tobias or not to be. I would inadvertently ask people, strangers, if they cheated on their spouse or significant others, would they tell them? Ninety-nine percent said they definitely would not tell. Then I asked most of the male patients that I came in contact with, "If your wife cheated on you would you forgive her? This time about ninety-nine and a half percent of them said, definitely not. I was really feeling like a dog now. I knew though that I had to make the trip to Virginia to tell Tobias what I did and to ask for his forgiveness. I had to face up to him and take the chance on him ending our marriage. Either way, I had to be honest with him. So, Malcolm and I made the trip to Virginia. Tobias had been transferred to another facility so the drive was longer. When Tobias came into the visiting room, he looked much thinner and worry lines creased his eyelids. I felt so bad that I had caused this. Anyway, after he sat down, I told him what I had done. He sat there at that table and cried like a baby. I cannot tell anyone how horrible I felt then for real. I started crying myself and Malcolm just sat there watching the two of us as we cried. After what seemed a long time Tobias finally spoke. He said, "Sweetheart, I forgive you. I don't think you really realize just how deeply in love I am with you. I know you're lonesome but what do you think about me? I'm just as lonesome as you are. Don't you think I want to be home with you and the children just as much as you want and need me to be there? When I said I do before God and our witnesses, I meant it. I mean to be faithful to you and our bed only." I just sat there nodding and crying as I held his hand with a death grip. He went on to say, "Sweetheart don't do that again. I love you but I won't go through this again." After I left the visiting room, I didn't feel much better. I still felt very guilty and seeing how much I had hurt Tobias made me feel even worse. He used to tell me that "To hurt you would only be hurting my self." I really didn't fully understand that statement then, but now I realized exactly what he meant.

So for quite a few years after that, I had to wrestle with my guilt and shame. Tobias was having his own personal wrestle as well. The affair came up very often it seemed. Whenever I would visit him, before the end of the visit came, I could count on him bringing it up again. When he wrote me, I could pretty much count on reading something about it. It wasn't helping me to heal by constantly hearing about it and it wasn't helping him to heal by not talking about it. I was very patient for a long while because I knew that I was responsible for his pain and mistrust. I also knew that if he was humble enough to forgive me, he would never have this trouble from me again. Just getting him to realize it was the issue. Finally, the last time he brought it up I said, "Sweetheart, I have been beating myself up over this for the past couple years and I'm tired of carrying the guilt around. If you say you've forgiven me, I wish you'd stop bringing it up at every available opportunity. I know this is your way of healing but it's not helping me to heal. If God has forgiven me and casts my sins as far from me as the east is from the west, I certainly wish you would." From that day to this one, Tobias has never mentioned it again. I'm sure he thinks about it from time to time but I've made it my business to show him that he is the only man on this earth for me. I lovingly and willingly go out of my way to show him and to let him know without any doubts, that I am his virtuous wife, woman, girlfriend, lover, best friend and anything else I need to be, for him and him only, for the rest of my earthly life.

I've asked God to make me be a virtuous, submissive wife to my husband. I realize that I cannot do anything without God's help but that I can do all things with it. When I talk to other women about being submissive to their husbands, some of the responses I get trouble my heart. They'll say things like,"Huh, I'm not getting up in the mornings fixing breakfast for no man and I'm not cooking all the time either. If I want to go out with my friends, I'm going and he can go where he wants to as well." I wonder if they and their significant others realize what a blessing it is to be able to wake up to your mate each day and go to sleep with them each night? Yet, most couples seem to take it for granted. I feel that if your man loves the Lord and puts Him first in his life, he will have that same love for his wife and family. Therefore, he will not ask you do to anything that is not in the will of God, thus making it 1, 2, 3, easy for a wife to be submissive to her husband. This is something I had to learn the hard way and I try to share this with others so that they might avoid unnecessary heartache. Hopefully, some of the women, and men, will embrace this concept.

Chapter 46

I came home from work one evening. I had stopped to check the mail box before coming home. In it was a card from Tyrone Jr. It was a Mother's Day card to be exact. On the front of the card read, Mom, You're a Blessing. On the inside of the card it read, God knew we'd all need mothers and, Mom, He even knew that of all the mothers everywhere our family would need you! Happy Mother's Day. Then he had written a poem on the inside of the card. It said:

"I Remember"

I remember the times that you did without, just to soothe our moans, groans and pouts,

You stayed in a home with a man that didn't care, just so your kids could have their father there.

I've seen you tired and stressed working hours on end and get up the next day and do it all again.

You were my father and mother when you had no spouse; and you still managed to move us from a trailer to a house.

You kept us a meal and many grocery bags to tote, even if it meant sending me to Mrs. Ruby's with a note.

Through all that we've done, said, and the many things we did, you never turned your back on a single one of your kids.

I love you like crazy for the mom that you have been; and if time allowed I know that you'd do it all again.

 P.S. I wrote this poem especially for the #1 woman in my life on her special day,

Love, your son

I just sat there in that car and cried like a baby let me tell you. I was moved beyond words. I was so touched and amazed at how this now, fine young man, had remembered so much about his childhood. I was so very humbled at his depiction of me as well. I now felt that all of my struggles had not been in vain or simply taken for granted. I sat there in the car for some time before going in the house and I read and reread this wonderful poem. The tears seemed to go on endlessly.

Michael continued to be incorrigible. I simply couldn't do anything with him. He continued to run with the wrong people. Where he was used to the guys back home acting like gangsters but who really were not true gangsters, here, he would soon realize, was another story entirely. In my efforts to help him, I talked with this very nice lady at the probation office named Mrs. Gull. I learned there was a program that I could get Michael into where he could earn his high school diploma as well as train in a military academy-like setting. The state would even pay for it. What a blessing this would be I thought. So we drove to Macon where the informative meeting took place. There, Michael was told beforehand that if he tested positive for drugs or if he displayed a negative attitude, one that could possibly rub off on another cadet, he would immediately be sent home. When we arrived back home, Mrs. Gull and I went shopping for Michael. She purchased him all the things he would need including black dress pants, a white shirt, black tie and black dress shoes. The morning that Michael was to leave came and I took him to the probation building where everyone was to meet. I kissed and hugged him goodbye and told him I loved him and I pleaded with him to do well with this. This was on a Monday morning. On Sunday morning, Michael was right back home. The people in Macon had put him on the bus right back home. Michael had taken a taxi from the bus station and came inside to get money from me to pay the taxi with. I was utterly disappointed. I asked him what happened and all he could find to say was, "I wasn't interested in that stuff." I immediately called and spoke with a Lieutenant. He told me that Michael's attitude was bad and he feared it would spread to the rest of the cadets so he had no choice but to send him home.

Michael continued running with the crowd that he was hanging with before he left. One night, I was awakened by a police officer banging on the door. I came downstairs to see what in the world was happening. There stood Michael with the police officer. The officer explained to me that Michael had been pistol whipped and had come to the police station fearing for his very life. I just backed up and sat on the stairs and started crying. Michael just stood there looking at me. I thanked the police officer for bringing Michael home and afterward, I looked at his head. It had a huge lump on it and it was bleeding but he didn't want to go to the hospital. I knew he was still afraid for his life. As it turned out, or as I later learned from one of Michael's associates named Tip, or so he was nicknamed, Michael had transacted some shady deals with these associates and they were going to kill him. Tip had been to my house on several occasions and I liked him. I treated him just like one of my own whenever he came around. He was a really big dude and he loved to eat and I loved to cook. So, whenever he would come around, I would feed him and enjoy seeing him enjoy my cooking. Anyway, Tip told me that these dudes were really mad with Michael and set out to take their revenge on him. Tip then said he knew the dudes and they respected him. He said he begged these guys not to kill Michael because he knew his mom and she was really a nice lady. He said he told the guys instead of killing Michael; just beat him up real bad. So that is what they did. I thank God for Tip to this very day. I knew I had been through a whole lot in my life, and I knew that God knew just how much I could bear. I really don't feel I could have dealt with losing a child though.

Cherylyn and I were back on speaking terms again. I was not fully comfortable with being around her though. She had always been a very sweet and kind daughter to me in the past. She had a heart as good as gold. She would give you her last if she thought you needed it. I decided to forgive her but it was still taking a while for me to regain that mother/daughter closesness that we shared before. Anyway, she was making a trip to Virginia and I thought it might be a good time for Michael to get out of Georgia and spend the weekend with her in Virginia. This would buy me some more thinking time as well as what to do with him next. He seemed glad to be leaving. When Cherylyn came back to Georgia on that Monday, Michael was not with her. I was worried sick and I asked her where he was. She said, "Momma, as soon as we got to Virginia, Michael got out of the car and ran and wouldn't come back. I don't know where he is." I soon learned that Michael had feared for his life so much that he had chosen to stay in Virginia. He managed to get himself locked up again as well. I felt he did this on purpose so as not to have to come back to Georgia because he knew that it wouldn't have been long before I'd be coming to get him. This time I learned, Michael had been placed in an adult jail while awaiting bed space in a juvenile detention center. He was going to turn 16 in a couple months and I was very concerned for his safety while placed with adults. There was really nothing I could do about it but worry and I was so sick and tired of worrying.

Michael was finally moved to a juvenile facility and spent a year there. He managed to get his GED while there and I received nothing but good reports on him from his counselor. I was very proud of him but I couldn't help but to wonder why it was that he could do so well with direct supervision from a stranger but would not listen to a word his own mother said. While there he wrote me a poem as well. It was a very sad poem to me. It read:

"I Wonder What God Thinks"

My life hasn't been the best, it started with robbing and stealing plus putting souls to rest.
I Wonder What God Thinks
How could my mom be a single parent and raise a young growing man?
My father was never there, that's why I hurt so bad.

God never left my side, however, I failed to follow his plans and the rules he set for me to abide.

He gives me chance after chance, still I don't hear Him. So he put my life on hold, only for me to fear Him.

Going from jail to jail, state to state, killing myself with drugs at a slow rate, still wondering will God allow me to see those pearly gates.

I Wonder What God Thinks

I know that I have to straighten myself and clear my personal slate; God please don't give up on me. I hear you loud and clear, I want to be a child of God now and throughout these last and evil years.

So many times I should have been dead but Your plans for me are bigger than that.

Thank you God, I'm so glad you delivered me from a lot of things, some I'm afraid to say,

But Lord I'll follow as long as you lead the way, Now I can be a good father to my daughter and teach her your laws and warn her of the games that Satan will play.

God, you are my father so in you I trust and have faith,

Please don't forsake me not even on my last and dying day.

I'm finished now but before I go I still would like to know, What does God think…

After reading it, I wondered just how much turmoil and trouble my child had been through. I felt really sad in my spirit. I was glad to know that I had raised my children in the fear and admonition of God and they knew He would never leave them.

When it came time for him to be released, I wrote a letter

to his counselor and told her that I would not take him back home with me. I told her that I loved him dearly and I would always love him but I just didn't see how I could help him. I let her know that I've tried countless times to help Michael, all to no avail. I said it was now time for Michael to help himself. Michael didn't know what to think of this. He was very upset but so was I. So, Michael was held over a couple of months while they gave me time to change my mind. It worked. After reading his letters about how much he had been through that I didn't even have a clue about and how he'd always felt like I never loved him, I felt bad for him. I couldn't see how in the world he felt this way but his little guilt trip worked like magic anyway.

John Lee had started attending this church that was next to our apartment complex. In all of the churches we had attended before, even in our little church back home, all of the members took a liking to John Lee and this church was no different. There was just something very special about him. Anyway, he ran home from church one day and he was bubbling over. He said, "Momma, I found us a house. It's a really nice house too." I said, "John Lee, what on earth are you talking about?" He went on to tell me that a nice lady in the church told him that her father had gotten sick and she was going to rent the house out. I called the lady whose name was Marla. She made an appointment for me to come to see the house. When I arrived at the house, I was surprised to find that it was directly across the street from the apartment complex. Even though it was in such close proximity, it was like the two places were worlds apart. Where the apartment complex was noisy all of the time and just as busy as it was noisy, here just across the street in this neighborhood, the houses were very nice and the neighborhood was very quiet and very well kept. This certainly was a blessing and a dream come true. I jumped at the opportunity to rent it from her. She even left the dining room furniture and a bedroom fully furnished. She said that she wanted John Lee to have that bedroom. He was just as thrilled as Malcolm and I were. It all worked out so perfectly. My lease was up and I was able to move into this very nice home without any issues with breaking the lease. What a blessing it was to be away from that hell of a home and apartment environment.

Chapter 47

The juvenile probation officer came to inspect my home again. It was a lovely home so he couldn't say anything except that it was adequate. I did not miss any time from work going to Virginia to pick Michael up this time; instead, I sent him bus fare. John Lee, Malcolm and I picked him up from the bus terminal and we were all very glad to see him. In the year that he had been away, I learned that every one of those guys, with the exception of Tip, had been murdered or incarcerated. I think Michael was relieved to know that. He looked a little shaken when I drove to our new house, I suppose because it was in the same area as the apartments we lived in before he left. He visibly relaxed when we drove in the garage of the new house. He was even more relaxed when he realized that this house and area was just like being in a whole different world. Mrs. Gull and another very nice man managed to have his juvenile records sealed so that it would not affect him getting a job or going into the military. I told Michael I thought the military would be an excellent opportunity for him, especially after seeing how well he functioned in a structured, well-disciplined environment. He said he would look into it but he never did. He really didn't do much of anything for a while. Even though he seemed to mature slowly, I began to see a definite change in him. Where before he was wild and could not seem to keep still for very long, now he was focusing on getting a job and settling down. I was so glad of that and so proud of him.

I will never forget one Thanksgiving holiday. Mother, Jamie and Tobias' oldest brother Walt Jr. had come down to spend the holidays with us. When they were about to leave, Michael asked to say a prayer before they left for the long drive home. I have been in church all of my life but I have never heard a finer prayer. Michael's sincerity touched us all that day. Mother and I were weeping after this wonderful prayer. My knees became very weak and I had to lean again the wall for support. It was then that I knew I didn't have to worry about Michael again and that he would surely be just fine, no matter what he would have to go through in his life. Michael knew how to communicate with the Lord. It was confirmed that day.

John Lee and Malcolm continued to do well in school. John Lee stayed active in the church as well. He loved to go with the church to the missions and to visit less fortunate areas to help people. He had a real talent with helping those that were underprivileged. John Lee graduated from school the following year and decided to go into the Army. We were all somewhat shocked that he chose this but I was very proud of him nonetheless. Malcolm did so well in school until he was chosen from a drawing to attend a magnet school. What an honor this was. He attended the magnet school for high achievers and remains in the program to this day. He was recognized with the honor of Who's Who Among Outstanding Middle School Students not so long ago. He was also recognized by the People to People Student Ambassador Programs and was invited to study abroad for the summer. As always, the money was an issue so he was not able to attend. He was somewhat upset about it but he understood that his mama just couldn't afford it. Malcolm has always been such a mature little person and he has grown to be quite a fine young man. Before I started writing this book I asked him how he felt about it. I told him that his friends would know that his father was an inmate. He simply responded, "Mom, I love my dad. I have the coolest dad in the whole world. If my friends stop associating with me simply because of that, they were never my friends anyway. I'll be better off knowing that."

Cherylyn and I have resolved our differences and have become closer than we were before. Despite her behavior earlier, she has always been a good hearted person. She has always been willing to help anyone that she thought needed it. She now sees that it isn't easy providing for yourself and a little one who is depending on you as well, and I think she respects me more now.

Chapter 48

This would be Tobias' 3rd time going before the parole board. This particular year, we decided that we should hire an attorney or someone in that capacity that would represent him. So, that is what I did. I worked a lot of extra shifts at the agency to pay for Mrs. Withers' services. The families of the inmates could come and sit before a member of the board to represent the inmate and share their reasons why they felt the inmate was ready for release. This was only allowed once in so many years. Well this year, after hiring Mrs. Withers and sharing with her all of Tobias' accomplishments and numerous commendation letters, as well as, the paperwork showing that Tobias had not had one single infraction on his record in the past 5 years, Tobias and I, as well as Mrs. Withers, felt confident that this would be his year. I called his mother so that she could be there with us as well. Doll and I drove up to Virginia all night so that we would be there the next day for this hearing. The hearing date was November 6th. When we arrived in Richmond at the office, we were met there by Mother and her wonderful husband Jamie. With them were Tobias's sister, Toni and his youngest brother Marc. Mrs. Withers was there as well. We waited a while for the meeting to commence. Once we were granted entry to the meeting, we entered this room and took our seats. Only four people other than Mrs. Withers were allowed to be inside of this room so Jamie and Toni waited for us outside. Before the meeting started, there was a lady there that introduced herself as Mrs. Silvers. She said she was one of the parole board members and she would be presiding over this meeting today. Then she went on to say that her own daughter had been the victim of a heinous crime some time back where she had been raped and murdered. I immediately thought to myself, "In light of this information, just how objective can this woman be when deciding whether or not to allow an inmate to be released from prison to be given a second chance at life." Still, I sat there and listened to her talk. Finally she gave each of us a chance to speak and we all spoke on Tobias' behalf. Mrs. Withers spoke first. Firstly, she provided Mrs. Silvers with the arrest records and court documents showing why Tobias was initially incarcerated the first time, then the documentation showing his offenses that led to his second incarceration. She then shared all of Tobias' good reports, his infraction free status and the commendation letters with Mrs. Silvers. A packet including all of the commendation letters and his infraction free status had been personally prepared by me and mailed to all five of the parole board members before the hearing as well. Mrs. Silvers appeared to be listening contently and with genuine concern. Just before the meeting was concluded, the question was posed to Mrs. Silvers about the process of deciding parole status and the time frame of the decision. She said, "The board will have to look at all of the information in his institutional files and then we will have to notify the victim(s) that were involved in his crime.

This process takes about a month. The victim(s) then has a month to respond with their input. So, all in all, we're looking at anywhere from 30-60 days with 60 days being the most time before a decision will be rendered." After this meeting was concluded, Mrs. Silvers stood in the doorway as we all walked out. As we walked past her, she gave us each a very firm handshake while making direct eye contact with us.

After Doll and I said our goodbyes to Tobias' family, we went to a nearby restaurant to eat. Doll said to me, "I don't think this Mrs. Silvers was genuine one bit. She had the coldest, darkest eyes I've ever seen. Her looking concerned and that tight handshake at the end didn't fool me one bit." I didn't say anything but I was very troubled in my spirit. After eating we drove back to Georgia.

The very next evening Tobias called me. He said, "Sweetheart, I have been denied parole again." I could hear it in his voice that he was very downtrodden. I couldn't believe my ears. I said, "Sweetheart, that can't be. We were just in Virginia on yesterday and in talking with Mrs. Silvers, she said the decision process would take anywhere from 30-60 days." Sure enough, Tobias sent me the paperwork in the mail and sure enough, he had been denied parole. Sure enough, the paperwork was dated November 6th. So, I knew that Doll had been correct in her assumption. The decision not to grant Tobias parole had already been decided, probably even before we wasted our time and money to drive there. If I had any doubts that Tobias was exaggerating when talking about the unfairness and underhandedness of the parole board and the system in general, I certainly had first-hand knowledge now for myself. I, right then and there, lost all faith in the parole board and the system. I decided then that I would put and keep my trust where it should have been all along, in God.

Tobias and I wrote letters anyway letting the Department of Corrections and the parole board know that we were well aware that we had been given the shaft. I wrote letters to the governor and the department of public safety as well. I never received a response from either of these departments. Tobias filed a complaint against the parole board's decision and it was decided that the board would reconsider it. Tobias and I knew that this was just another big joke and sure enough, the board's decision still came back as denied "Due to the serious nature of the crime." That was the most ridiculous reason for denying parole to Tobias or anyone else for that matter. Would the nature of the crime ever change, serious or otherwise? I thought it was the individual who was supposed to change anyway, not the crime. I now viewed the system and the parole board as working hand in hand to further impose their own form of punishment although the judge and jury had already done so.

Chapter 49

It was Valentine's Day again, and again, it was Tobias' and my anniversary. Although his spirits were down trodden, he was determined to continue to do well. He would always say that the children and I were his focus. He would continue to focus on us and not his environment because he would not let anything or anyone stand in his way of coming home. He had been up for parole six times and turned down six times, all for the same reason, "The serious nature of the crime." He had been transferred to a level 2 facility and worked as a barber. He still remained infraction free and had been for 8 years now. None of this apparently mattered to anyone other than Tobias, me and the children. Still, I was determined to stand by my man under any and all circumstances.

I was coming home from work and again I checked the mailbox. In it was a letter from Tyrone Jr. He was doing so well in prison. Whenever I would visit him the officers would ask me, "What on earth is he doing in here? He certainly doesn't belong here. He's never given any of us one minute's trouble." I would just smile and say thanks. The facility where Tyrone

Jr. was housed had very nice officers and they treated the families with humanity and kindness. That really meant a lot to me. Tyrone Jr. had completed several college computer courses and had been chosen as the instructor's assistant. I was so very proud of him. My, how he had matured and grown into such a fine young man during his incarceration! He could have made a bad situation worse; instead, he chose to make a bad situation better. Once inside the house, when I opened the letter, it was another poem he had written to me. Malcolm was standing by my side when I opened it. When he saw that it was another poem he asked, "Mom do you want me to read it for you?" He knew that a huge waterfall was imminent. So, I handed the poem to Malcolm and he read:

Momma Can Ya Hear Me?

For nine months you carried me with tender love and care,

Through childhood you guided me in times of happiness and despair.

Momma Can Ya Hear Me?

You always made sure that we had, even if you had not,

That's why I chose this Valentine's Day to say momma I love ya a lot.

Momma Can Ya Hear Me?

We've been through a lot without a doubt, our journey hasn't been a breeze,

But God tells me in the bible that with every struggle there will come ease.

Momma Can Ya Hear Him?

Momma I would be lost without ya, and I commend you
on a job well done;

And one thing that ya must know with all sincerity is that
it's a blessing to be your son.

Momma Do Ya Feel Me?

Momma I hope ya heard me because I mean every word
I just said,

But if any day ya have any doubts just bring to mind the
poem that you just read.

Momma I Hope Ya Heard Me!!!

Happy Valentine's Day

Malcolm was correct in his assumption. The waterworks
were turned on in a big way. Even now as I write, I cannot
help but to sit here and cry. I cry, not out of sadness, but out
of gratitude and thankfulness that Tyrone Jr. would think of
me in this way. I truly thank God for my life, my family and
all that He has brought us through. I cannot give Him enough
praise!

Chapter 50

Time seemed to be moving quickly. It was time for another parole year for Tobias, his 7th to be exact. He and I had long since stopped writing letters to the parole board before his hearings. We felt that it was just a waste of time and postage. Tobias told me on several occasions that he felt there was something in his institutional file that prevented him from being granted parole. I now knew better than to doubt his intuitions. I'd had my own first hand experience with them and so I agreed that he was probably correct. So about two months before the hearing was scheduled, around October 10th, Tobias requested a copy of his records. He was charged for the costs of making the copies and the money was immediately withdrawn from his account, a total of $30.40. He did not receive these records however until after his interview with an examiner representing the parole board. He said he was called to pick up his copies and when he arrived to where he had to pick them up from, he was told by the nurse that he could not have his mental health notes. He said he was totally floored when he was told that he had mental health notes. He said he then requested copies of all of these "mental health notes" and was charged another $8.40. He said the money was not taken out of his account until nearly a month later on December 13th. He said that on December 18th, he received a total of 46 pages, 15 of them being duplicates pages. He says as he read the documents he found some very disturbing information.

At least three different psychologists with whom he had never spoken to or ever even seen had concluded that he had a diagnosis of Antisocial Personality Disorder. He said the source of these psychologists' information according to the documents was "My Medical/Mental Health Record and the inmate". He says that a B. G. Hill, on 6-2 diagnosed him with Antisocial Personality Disorder, a C. Wash on 12-22 concluded the same without ever speaking to Tobias yet claims his/her information came from both Tobias and his record. Then on 4-28, he says a Don Kell made the same diagnosis but unlike the other two psychologists, based his information solely on the records. Further, in the documentation that Tobias was able to send to me, a M. M. Conner documented that per a Ms. Watts' request; he/she completed a mental health screening. He says copies of this were then circulated to a C. Daley, the Chief Social Worker and the Regional Mental Health Director. All of this is entirely a lie and I have the documentation safely tucked away to prove that it is. I wonder if any of these medical professionals realized the serious consequences surrounding false documentation when they were all, obviously, up to no good. Tobias had really been railroaded big time.

Then, to make bad matters worse, if it could be worse, Tobias ran across a letter in his file as well. It was written by none other than Mr. McKine and date 12-21. He wrote: "At the time of the injury I did not experience symptoms which caused me concern; therefore, I remained at work that day and completed the necessary AIR and disciplinary form. Mr. Hines was charged with "Assault upon any Person" 105 charge. At the time of the assault I did not believe I needed further medical attention other than what was rendered by the GRCC medical department personnel; however, about 3 weeks later I began to experience black specks and blurred vision in my right eye. Upon going to the ophthalmologist and inquiring about the cause of this problem I was told that there was a casual relationship between my head injury a few weeks earlier and the development of what was termed retinal tears in my right eye. As a result of this I underwent laser treatment. About a month later I needed surgery for a detached retina in my right eye. Due to the seriousness of my injuries I filed criminal charges against Mr. Hines for simple assault in Greensville Circuit Court in Emporia, Va. On December 21, after a brief trial, Mr. Hines was found Not Guilty of the assault charge. Since the assault against me I do fear for my personal safety thus I am requesting that Mr. Hines not be housed in a prison where I am employed. I am requesting that Mr. Hines be transferred to another facility, such as, Augusta Correctional Center to lessen the likelihood of him coming into physical contact with me." He then craftily sent a copy of this letter to the warden, the parole board and others in the upper echelon of the Department of Corrections. What Mr. McKine neglected to include in his letter were the facts that had been revealed in the trial; that he had retinal tears prior to this incident and had been receiving treatment at this Retinal Association and that he'd had diminishing vision problems for over 10 years! It is no wonder how Mr. McKine was able to make the statement "I'll personally see to it that you do every day of your sentence" to Tobias after the trial with such surety. He had laid the ground work to get his own vengeance since the facts revealed during Tobias' trial and the outcome of it was obviously not what he'd expected. At some point on the same day after the conclusion of the trial, Mr. McKine wrote this letter and circulated it. What is so amazing is that from the time of this incident, which occurred in February, Mr. McKine continued to work at the same institution where Tobias was housed. He worked right there for the next ten months, sometimes crossing paths with Tobias during his daily routine. It was not until after the trial, ten months later, and after the "Not Guilty" verdict, that Mr. McKine developed this "fear" for his personal safety, truly amazing indeed. All of this makes me wonder just who really needs rehabilitation. I knew that I could not afford to hire an attorney to look into this gross injustice but I didn't worry about it. I knew that God had made so many ways for me before when things seemed utterly hopeless and I refused to start doubting Him now. God didn't always work things out in the time frame in which I expected Him to, but when He worked them out; He was always right on time! This time was no different.

So, it has been a wonderful, quite adventurous, sometimes painful, disappointing, frustrating 15 years since my first meeting Tobias at that pill window. This Valentine's Day we will have been married for 15 years. I was thinking just the other day, "We'll be married for 15 years very soon and we've never seen each other naked." What a mess. I had to laugh at that myself. I have watched as Tobias grew and matured into something very special indeed. He has watched me grow and mature as well. He has sat by and observed in silence and with a feeling of complete helplessness as I've gone through many, many of life's struggles while he was unable to help me or be there for me. I've been right by his side through his struggles as well, and his struggles have been many indeed.

Yet, through it all, we remain steadfast in this marriage. I believe that is the key in life, the word "through." If we never go through anything, we could not reach our blessings on the other side of it. We both love the Lord and have put Him at the center of our lives and our marriage. The long journey, as Tyrone Jr. reminded me, hasn't been a breeze, but surely, with every struggle, there really has come ease. If the parole board never grants Tobias parole, it will only be four more years until he won't need them to grant him one thing. He will have paid his debt in full to society and them. With this said, I continue to wait patiently while growing in faith that soon, this will all be over. We will finally be afforded the opportunity of bringing this physical separation that exists between us to a close despite all odds. By God's grace and mercy, I feel that soon I won't have to say: "Been Married All My Life-Never Had a Husband."

About the Author

Shirley W. Hines was born and raised in a small city in Virginia. She spent the first thirty-nine years of her life there. She later moved to Atlanta, Georgia where she continues to reside. She is happily married and is the mother of five children and has three grandchildren. She is a nurse and has been for almost eighteen years. As a  young child, she always dreamed of becoming a nurse because she always had the desire to help people and to feel as though she were making a positive difference in their lives, no matter how large or small. She has always and continues to enjoy this profession.

Shirley was born the youngest of six children. Her father was a Bishop and her mother a Missionary. She was raised in the church atmosphere all of her early years and was raised in the fear and admonition of the Lord. Even though, as a child, she was not always happy about being raised in a strict, religious environment, now as a grown woman and a mother herself, she has come to appreciate her rearing as a child and her religious upbringing. She has, at many, many times in her life, had nothing else to rely on except those same principles that were instilled in her as a child. Although she has made mistakes in the past, and continues to make mistakes even now, Shirley loves the Lord with all of her heart. She endeavors to let that love shine through in her everyday interactions with others.

Printed in the United States
76061LV00002B/643-651